Free Your True Self 1

Releasing Your Unconscious Defence Patterns

Free Your True Self 1

Releasing Your Unconscious Defence Patterns

ANNIE MARQUIER

FINDHORN
Press

© Annie Marquier 1998, 2000, 2003, 2005

First published in English by Findhorn Press in 2005
First published in French by Editions du Gondor in 1998

ISBN 1-84409-054-X

British Library Cataloguing-in-Publication Data.
A catalogue record for this book is available
from the British Library.

Translated from the French by Alain Groven
Edited by Shari Mueller
Cover design by Damian Keenan
Interior design by Thierry Bogliolo.

Printed and bound in the USA

Published by
Findhorn Press
305a The Park, Findhorn
Forres IV36 3TE
Scotland, UK
tel 01309 690582/fax 690036
info@findhornpress.com
www.findhornpress.com

CONTENTS

Introduction

We all seek joy and freedom in our lives. We know that these states of being spring more from within than from outside circumstances. The purpose of this book is to allow each of us to regain freedom from certain inner mechanisms that restrict our capacity for happiness, and transform them naturally into strengths and qualities. As a result of that inner shift, joy, peace and mastery will be far more readily accessible in our day to day existence.

These mechanisms refer to certain defence systems in the form of **5 basic structures that presently shape our unconscious**, on both a personal and collective level. These fundamental mechanisms of the psyche have become part of the human unconscious over thousands of years, and now form our common heritage. In their present state, they create dynamics that become major impediments to self expression and fulfilment, and to the creation of a truly satisfying life. On the other hand, we all have the opportunity to **transform them into positive dynamics that can enhance our chances of achieving full self-realisation**. In order for this to happen, the first thing we need to do is to identify them clearly and joyfully.

Joyfully indeed because these dynamics are only temporary hurdles that we are bound to overcome sooner or later. Instead of endlessly beating our heads against these limitations without knowing where they come from, thereby generating a great deal of hardship in our lives, we can transform them and free ourselves by first developing a clear awareness of their existence and their impact. What will then naturally emerge within us is a radiant energy, joy of living and freedom that will allow us to create and to truly celebrate our existence at all levels.

Through over thirty years of coaching people involved in conscious inner work, I have witnessed both the constricting effects of these dynamics and the real potential we all have of transcending these limitations. These are not merely philosophical inferences. They are based on a concrete observation of actual life experiences. For beyond our usual limitations, each of us carries great creative power and exceptional qualities that makes every one of us unique beings.

May this book help you to be in touch again with this powerful, wise and loving presence which already dwells in your heart, which will guide you wisely on your path towards happiness, love and freedom. May this book help you to free your True Self.

chapter 1

Know Thyself

If you can clearly know your prison,
you can design and plan your escape.
—Lazaris

1-1   A Loving Ideal vs. a Tough Reality

For thousands of years, great masters of wisdom have been extolling the highest virtues. We would love to live up to these wonderful teachings pointing the way to unconditional love, inner peace, serene detachment, clear awareness and so on, not only during a few special moments of meditation or inner practice, but in our day-to-day existence, our relationships, our professional lives, our personal and collective achievements in this world.

Yet despite our best intentions and however intense our aspiration to lead blissful lives may be, we often find ourselves overwhelmed with painful emotional reactions or very negative thoughts. We experience anxiety and stress rather than peace—frustration and anger rather than fulfilment. We tend to shut out a difficult world rather than open up to its beauty. Instead of living in love, we live in fear, which separates and destroys.

What do we make of such paradoxes dwelling within us? How can we achieve a state of being that reflects our deepest aspirations towards peace and joy?

As we become aware of this inner duality, the question that arises is why…why are we caught between this intense desire to be happy and such difficulty when we try to achieve this happiness in our daily lives? This question takes us straight to the oracle of Delphi: **"Man, know thyself and thou wilt know the Universe and the gods"**. Or in more modern terms: get to know your own inner dynamics so that you can master them and discover the ecstasy of true freedom.

But what do we mean by self-knowledge anyway? What link can there be between philosophy and some colleague's unpleasant behaviour at work, for example, or a friend's betrayal?

With no sense of the real source of our unpleasant inner states, we tend to look for causes in external circumstances, especially in other people. Or we cling to the hope that in time, things will get better (when we meet someone new, get another job, move to another location, retire, take a vacation, etc.), but meanwhile, we are still endlessly mired in highly unpleasant situations due to our lack of mastery.

And yet life can be infinitely more pleasant. From the moment we start to gain knowledge and mastery of our emotional and mental processes, and acquire a deeper understanding of ourselves and other people, our relationships become smoother, our creative capacity increases, our power is manifested, our health improves, and magic springs up in our lives.

Our lives change when we gain a better understanding and mastery of our nature, not because external circumstances have changed.

But how do we get to know and master our true nature?

1-2 Soul and Personality: The Musician and His Instrument

All of the teachings expounded in every cultural lineage remind us that we have a physical body, as well as emotions and thoughts, but that we are in essence "something else" that is endowed with all this. We will start here with the premise that this is known or intuitively felt by many. It is this essence of who we are, our true nature, or Higher Self, our "Soul"[1] —whatever word we use to refer to it— that bears all of the highest qualities (love, wisdom, peace of mind, creative power, vitality, joy of living, etc.) that we hunger for. It is that part of us which is the source of that powerful inner drive to attain bliss and inner freedom. And it is also that part of us which is endowed with the knowledge and wisdom required to actualise all that potential.

But then if we, in essence, carry this limitless potential, and if, in addition, we are familiar with all the right principles, why is it so difficult for us to integrate all this into our day-to-day existence? At this point, we need to realize that our limitations are not part of our essence. These limitations are found **in the instrument that makes the expression of that essence possible** in our world. This instrument is what we call our personality, or ego[2], a composite whole made up of our physical, emotional and mental bodies.

Our Higher Self *actually needs* this instrument in order to express itself in the phenomenal world. The ego has often been maligned or misunderstood as to its true purpose. It is quite useful however; indeed, it is absolutely necessary. On the other hand, if it is inadequate, damaged or unfinished, it can be the source of many limitations, and our essence cannot express the full quality of its potential.

At the level of the Higher Self, we can assume that man is perfect. The goal of the process of evolution, i.e. the goal of our very existence on this earth, is not to achieve a level of perfection which is already there, but rather to build an instrument (personality, ego) that is totally supple and responsive to the energy and to the will of the soul, so that we can manifest its perfection directly and concretely in this world.

We could compare the Higher Self to a brilliant, marvellously inspired and talented violinist. He obviously needs a violin (the personality) to express in perceptible form the beauty of the music he carries within himself. The ego or personality is the violin, but it is currently under construction: the body is not completely finished, the tuning pegs are not quite right, some strings are missing or out of tune. No matter how brilliant the violinist may be, there is no way for him to make beautiful music. No matter how perfect our Higher Self may be, it cannot as yet manifest all of its beauty, its richness and its power in this world.

Under such conditions, instead of despising this instrument or wanting to get rid of it as quickly as possible because it does, in fact, limit the full expression of our magnificence, what we have to do is lovingly take care of it, tune it, make needed adjustments and refine it so that it becomes a perfect instrument to express the will of our Higher Self. With this purpose in mind, if we intend to live our daily lives in peace, joy and inner freedom, we need to examine the workings of the instrument—its strong and weak points—in order to gain mastery in its use. Only then will we be able to experience true happiness.

1-3 The Source of Our Limitations

What is the cause of the shortcomings we find in the instrument? What is it about the instrument that prevents us from living in the state of peace, joy and inner freedom that is inherent in the will of our Higher Self and that we all long for? What is it that throws our emotional responses off course, scrambles our mental reactions, makes us so tired and generates such problems in our lives?

The word is spreading fast, in conventional psychology as well as in holistic approaches, that we carry within us the imprint of painful past experiences, both physical and psychological, that have not yet been integrated. These experiences have for the most part been "forgotten" at the conscious level, yet are all the more active at the unconscious level and they condition our physical, emotional and mental responses without our realising it.[3] Indeed, when we experienced these intense moments of stress, these fears or great pains, we stiffened and became locked in a natural response of self-protection. **At such times, specific memories were installed in relation to these situations**, memories that we still carry in active form in our unconscious. They are active because human beings recoil from suffering, and in our limited human condition, **we built unconscious defence systems based on these memories** in order to avoid possible suffering in the future. These are the mechanisms which, if not defused, continue to condition our lives without our knowing it, and prevent us from experiencing the beauty and power of our true nature.

Very briefly, the protective process goes like this: Every moment our unconscious—which is comparable to a powerful computer hooked up to radar—scans our environment to check whether there is any danger of a painful past situation recurring. Should there be anything remotely resembling a previously experienced situation, the system is activated so that we project the past situation onto the present one. We automatically react at all levels of our being as if we were again faced with this past situation, which usually has nothing to do with the present. Our perception of things and other people is thus highly distorted and our responses are completely inappropriate. Our actions, decisions and choices are greatly misled, while we remain totally unaware of what is truly going on. And this is something that happens on a constant basis. These automatic "protection" mechanisms are activated at the least incident of our day-to-day existence.

Yet all this goes on unnoticed: these systems of self protection are so deeply rooted in our unconscious that nothing in our daily lives will bring them to our attention. On the contrary, our daily experience, when caught in these automatic responses, only serves to reinforce them.

As long as these systems remain active, we live our lives like a blind captain taking to the sea without knowing the mechanisms that operate his ship. When the weather is fine, all goes relatively well. But as soon as he hits any kind of bad weather, the ship is tossed around every which way, strikes a reef, and begins to take on water. Our life becomes more and more stressful, our relationships break down, problems pile up all around us, with all the tensions and dissatisfactions they entail. We blame it all on the storm, of course, and we desperately cling to the lifelines, hoping that the ship will not sink and that good weather will soon be upon us. Such is life; the barometer is not locked on high, and the situations encountered in our lives are not always ideal. Life is no picnic; there is chaos rather than peace, suffering rather than well being, misunderstanding rather than sharing, powerlessness rather than creative drive, for we have lost all power to direct the course of our life.

Under such conditions, if we wish to regain a sense of balance and mastery, it will be necessary to recognise the state we are in, and do what is required in order to learn to take control of our ship. Once the captain regains a clear, undistorted view of things, and is no longer (metaphorically) blinded by stuff from the past, it becomes easy for him to steer the ship through all kinds of weather, safely and even joyfully, for he now is the master of his ship.

Thus, by learning to recognise our unconscious defence patterns which strongly condition our responses and prevent us from seeing reality as it is, we make it possible for us to regain a clearer, more accurate perception of our life, and to liberate our power to create an unfettered, more blissful existence.

1-4 Understanding our Defence Mechanisms: The Five Major Structures of the Unconscious

There was a long held belief that the content of the human unconscious was mysterious, or at least very complex. One tended to avoid digging too deep into that Pandora's box, being somewhat wary of what may lie hidden there. Only people having great difficulty coping and who were more or less dysfunctional were allowed to ponder such questions, if possible with the help of a trained specialist.

In reality, however, the fact of the matter is a lot simpler. **We all carry unconscious mechanisms that are part of the human condition**. These mechanisms are an inherent part of the evolutionary process. In light of new approaches in modern psychology, and of the teachings of the Ageless Wisdom, we can now demystify the unconscious, stop being afraid of it, acknowledge its usefulness, and make it our friend.

In the course of this book, we learn to identify **five major unconscious defence patterns** stemming from five specific types of painful experiences that are common to the entire human race. We will observe how these patterns shape our daily behaviours; they will also be called "character structures" in the remainder of this book. The description of actual life experiences I have witnessed in my work, will make it easier to grasp the concrete reality of these patterns, the significant impact they have on our life, and our potential to transcend them. The specific characteristics related to each of these structures of the unconscious will be presented in detail and illustrated with a number of examples. It will be easy for us to identify them in ourselves and in people around us. This will be an opportunity for a wonderful breakthrough towards a deeper, more loving understanding of ourselves and others.

1-5 In the Flow of the Evolutionary Process

Even though we may recognise a lot of our familiar behaviours as we go through the description of these confining patterns, we should remember that **these mechanisms are not who we are**. They are part of our instrument, and they do not change the fact that we are perfect in essence. Our task is simply to do what is needed so that this instrument can perform at its best.

We should also remember that having these mechanisms within our makeup does not make us bad people. These **dynamics are merely the expression of an evolutionary process that is built this way**, just as scaffolding is used in the construction of a house. This is very valuable equipment that is absolutely necessary for a time. However, it becomes rather unsightly, cumbersome and even dangerous when the house is practically finished.

Many of us have now reached a level of evolution such that certain ego mechanisms, which provided valuable protection for a while, have now become not only awkward and useless, but they actually hinder our access to the house. It is time for us to become free of all the mechanisms that prevent our enjoyment of this beautiful inner house that was built over time. We are ready to welcome the "inner Master", so that what we are in essence, our true Self, can be revealed.

1-6 Our Next Step: The Need for Consciousness

Using our day-to-day experiences as a starting point, we will embark on a grand journey through our unconscious, which is not nearly as mysterious and complex as we might think. We can even take pleasure in this journey. Along the way, we will certainly recognise a number of more or less pleasant situations that we encounter on a daily basis. But we will be able to distance ourselves from these situations, and even sometimes bring in a little humour to lighten things up, as we will have a better understanding of the deep-rooted mechanisms underscoring these situations. This greater awareness of ourselves will open our hearts to healing and compassion, and provide us with an ample measure of peace of mind.

By recognising these unconscious defence patterns which made us act like automatons and lose control of our lives, we will be able to free ourselves from their influence and live out each day with more of the beauty and authenticity of our True Self.

**Let's tune our violin
and free our True Self
so we can play wonderful, loving and joyful music
in all areas of our lives.**

---

[1] In this book, the terms "Self" (with a capital "S"), "Higher Self" or "soul" will be used interchangeably to describe the essence of who we truly are.

[2] In this book, the words "ego" and "personality" will be used interchangeably.

[3] Nearly a century ago, Freud blazed a new trail towards understanding the human psyche. Since then, a number of in-depth studies on the mechanisms of the brain have given us a clearer and more precise view of these dynamics of the unconscious. See *Free Your True Self 2* and *The Master in Your Heart* by Annie Marquier.

chapter 2

Character Structures: An Overall Presentation

Today is Helen's birthday, and she invited several of her friends to celebrate the event at her home. A buffet is laid out by the pool and there is music and dance to liven things up. Her brother James has just returned from a three-year stay in African bush country. He doesn't know anyone, and from his perch on a stool, he watches all this human wildlife in action. There is Jean, Helen's boss. Why did she invite him? To begin with, he was the only one to arrive exactly at the appointed time, and nothing was ready. Perhaps this is the reason for his bad mood, for he has worn a cold and distant look on his face from the moment he got here. He looks so stiff that you would think he swallowed a broomstick. When people started dancing, he moved closer to the bar, his gaze fixed upon his drink. There was no way he would move from that position. In fact he left shortly thereafter. In sharp contrast, there is a pretty girl who can't stop smiling at everyone. She is attractive, and one cannot help but wonder what she would look like without the smile stretching the corners of her mouth. Besides this, James would be curious to know what the lady with the sad and tense expression on her face is sharing with this other lady, a friend of hers apparently. She really looks exhausted, hardly able to stand on her feet for the rest of the evening. He chats with Helen: it seems that one of her friends has just played a very mean trick on her, and she is having a hard time getting over it. In fact she scowls at just about every male in sight. Cousin Charles, on the other hand, looks bright and chirpy. Of course he is fully enjoying the generous catered buffet that Helen ordered, and he must have consumed an incredible amount of everything on the table. He wanders from one platter to another, while never straying far from the young woman who came with him and who seems tethered to his side. Helen's fiancé isn't eating very much at all, except maybe a few radishes. He is a vegetarian, and doesn't drink alcohol. Tall and thin as a beanstalk, he seems totally lost in his fantasies. No one dares to disturb him. In one corner of the room, an intense conversation is underway between Helen's father, a retired engineer, and a yoga teacher, each trying to prove to the other that his philosophy is right on the mark. Thank goodness there is Marco, a colleague of Helen's, to add a little zest to the evening. There is no getting around him: a great talker, with a greater capacity to absorb liquor, whose stories and jokes strike everyone within earshot, he is also very handsome, and every woman's eyes are upon him; a remarkable fellow, the life of the party. Everyone, and others who happen to join the group, seem to have gathered there for entertainment. Yet beyond the masks, James senses tension, stress, worry, and suffering.

In this scenario, anyone can recognise certain familiar attitudes for which there are an infinite number of variations. Why do human beings unconsciously behave in such automatic ways? Why is it so difficult to tune into genuine joy, peace and fulfilment? Where do these stereotyped attitudes and others that limit our capacity for joyful living come from?

Helen's friends, like most of us, are caught in very specific ego mechanisms. Their unconscious defence patterns are controlling their lives without their knowing it.

2-1 An Overview of Character Structures

We shall closely examine the **five unconscious defence systems**, generating five types of behaviour, which could also be described as five major **character structures** related to the ego. These will cover most types of human behaviour at the personality level. As we shall see, our ego is not very original.

Among all the descriptions and diagnostic tables found in the world of psychology today, we find an inspiring starting point in Wilhelm Reich, an Austrian psychiatrist whose approach has been widely used, with many variations, by many other schools of psychiatry.[1] My intention here is not to use all of Reich's approach, but his basic classification system. I have taken the liberty to adapt, expand, modify and enrich this system in the light of my professional experience, and present a broader perspective which encompasses the evolution of humanity.[2]

We have thus created our own approach, knowing that just as there are innumerable ways of describing a landscape, there are many ways of describing the complexity of the human unconscious. The richness of the human psyche can be described from several viewpoints. We find the same complexity here, in the sense that each individual carries within him a combination of these five structures, a combination that is uniquely his. In addition, each person will tend to express more of the weaknesses

> The five character structures describe five major ego dynamics, at the conscious and unconscious levels, which affect each of us to varying degrees, depending on one's history and one's level of evolution.

or more of the strengths of these structures, depending on the level of ego mastery already attained by each soul. I have chosen to work from this perspective, for it provides one of the most accurate reflections of the psychological reality that I want to describe, and it fosters new depths of awareness regarding our daily behaviours. Furthermore, it can be easily harmonised with other approaches[3], and can enrich the other approaches with a deeper understanding of certain aspects of human nature.

These structures will be presented in a spirit of observation without judgement. The only subject of evaluation will be the extent to which these mechanisms generate hardship and suffering, and how they can be a source of peace and freedom.

We must insist on this neutral attitude, for truly the behaviours stemming from these different structures are neither harmonious nor desirable (pride, selfishness, fear, aggressiveness, irresponsibility, manipulation, arrogance, coldness). In fact, they have often been regarded as "immoral" or "bad". In general, we tend to blame those who exhibit these behaviours. By shedding light on their source, we will be in a far better position to understand them in ourselves as well as in others, to stop blaming ourselves or those around us, and to recognise the fact that, beyond these reactions, there is **an authentic being trying to find its genuine identity, its source, its freedom**. It is important to keep this in mind throughout our study of these structures, so as not to use this information to become even more judgmental.

It is also worth remembering that, even if all of these past experiences and this stiffening of the personality have generated, and continue to generate, a great deal of suffering, this is not "unfortunate". Even though our limited consciousness is geared towards the avoidance of suffering, and thus finds certain aspects of this dynamic revolting, they were appropriate in the broader context of our evolution.

2-2 General Comments Regarding These Structures

Before we get into a specific description of each structure, let us mention a few general points which apply to all of them.

1) Each personality is a mix of several structures

As we go through the description of these structures, we will probably realise that we carry within us a mix of several structures. Since the history of humanity is embedded within our personal history, we carry all five of these structures, to varying proportions, according to certain characteristics of our evolutionary past as well as our soul's intention for this present lifetime. We shall therefore find certain aspects of our personality in each structure.

It is interesting to note the structure that is most active within us, the one that seems, for the time being at least, to bring the greatest constraints in our daily life and which determines most of our behaviours. Our ego will buck very strongly against this realisation, for it builds its very identity on the basis of these structures. A great deal of humility and sincerity is required in order to accept what we see as reality, to be able to see ourselves as we really are, and to see our mechanisms at work.

If, as a result of inner work, we manage to soften a structure to a sufficient extent, two dynamics will emerge.

• On the one hand, the structure becomes a source of creative energy, for it is imbued with all the positive elements generated as a result of learning through past experiences which have now been fully integrated. It enhances the personality and becomes **a vehicle of expression of specific qualities of the soul** which were previously blocked or adulterated in the structure.[4]

I will make a point of mentioning these qualities so as to see the positive aspects in these structures, even if they appear constricting at first glance. This may also give us a more precise idea of the potential within each of us, and motivate us to do the inner work required to unleash the beauty and the richness of our soul and to foster its fuller expression in the world.

- On the other hand, given the fact that the baggage accumulated in the course of our evolutionary process is so varied, we have had ample occasion to build complex defence systems. The ego is the sum of these different structures which were built in the past. For this reason, whenever we mange to free ourselves from one of them, another one generally emerges which constitutes the next phase of our work towards inner liberation. So it is quite normal to recognise a part of ourselves in more than one structure.

2) Our description of the different structures will be highly typical

Even if we are deeply entangled in a particular structure, we do not necessarily manifest all of its aspects, for a variety of reasons. First of all, each of us has his/her own particular history, and reacts on the basis of the complexity of his/her past. Also, our personality is composed of several overlapping structures, and this further creates nuances. Finally, depending on individual levels of evolution, a structure may be very rigid, taken to its extreme form, generating very constricting behaviours, or it may already be quite flexible, and as such a good medium of manifestation for the soul. Between these two extremes, there is a whole spectrum of varying degrees. Yet despite these nuances, we shall see that a general description is highly revealing, and that it can foster major realisations regarding our behaviour mechanisms.

3) Different levels of evolution lead to different types of behaviours

Depending on one's level of evolution, these personality structures can generate three types of behaviours:

✓ **First type:** these include behaviours directly generated by a totally rigid defence system. This is where a person has a low level of self-awareness, and where the personality is dominated by the lower mind. In such cases, the structure is a source of typical behaviours which are highly constricting and sometimes destructive, both for the affected individual and for others.

✓ **Second type:** these refer to behaviours generated by one's efforts to disengage oneself from a defence system, indicating a more highly developed state of awareness, as is the case with people who are involved in a conscious process towards a greater level of fulfilment.

✓ **Third type:** these refer to behaviours generated by the qualities of a defence system, which has been softened and transformed, and has thus become a system of expression and service. This is the case with people whose consciousness is ever more highly developed.

For each structure, we will begin with a description of the first two stages which apply to most of us, to varying degrees, at this stage of our history, and then proceed with a description of the qualities of the structure once it has been transformed and has become a supple instrument subject to the will of the Self.

2-3 A Six-Point Presentation Format

This format will be roughly the same for each structure, i.e.:

I – One or two stories illustrating certain typical behaviours in everyday living which stem from that particular structure. These are simple but concrete examples, which are very revealing and give a general idea of the structure. The behaviour patterns will then be described in greater detail in point V.

II – Past life experiences from which this structure originates. Three aspects must be noted here:

First, we must remember that it is not necessary to "believe" in past lives in order to be able to use the information. The aim of this section is not to prove anything in this respect. The paragraphs relating to past lives can simply be ignored or taken as working hypotheses. One can choose to have these memories go back to early childhood, which is a generally accepted fact, or choose the broader perspective of a resonance with a more distant past.

Second, I will generally present sources other that those springing from the present lifetime as part of an individual's direct personal past life experience. This is for the sake of keeping our presentation simple. But bear in mind that the issue can be approached from a broader perspective. As I noted in the preceding chapter, what may appear as a past life experience can also stem from one's ancestral lineage, or even from the broader pool of the collective unconscious colouring the content of one's personal unconscious. When it comes down to unravelling the structure, both the personal and collective aspects can be considered indifferently, as they generate the same mechanisms and can be worked on in the same way.

There is no clear boundary separating the personal and the collective unconscious, as it depends on the individual's level of evolution. Ultimately, when we get to the point of living in the consciousness of the Self, personal history will no longer be a factor. We will be living in such a state of unity that the entire history of human consciousness will be ours. For now, we are still at a point where our responsibility is to work on a personality as an instrument of manifestation, and in this context it is useful to look at things from a relatively personal vantage point. (Referring to the analogy described in Chapter 5 of *Free Your True Self 2*, we must first work on the room assigned to us.)

Third, trying to find out about our past life histories is not what will ultimately allow us to know whether a structure is active or not in our personality.

Indeed, the memories that were generated at that time are linked to external circumstances, but their impact depends on the way the personality reacted to these circumstances, i.e. on the individual's level of evolution, and on the level of mastery gained by that person's soul over his/her personality. Personal history is therefore not an essential factor. By working on the energetic level, we can defuse active memories without consciously reconnecting with the history that generated them.

On the other hand, it will be easy to recognise a structure, in ourselves or in our clients if we are involved in a helping relationship, by simply observing behaviours or the practical limitations that affect a personality on a daily basis. The description of behaviour characteristics (point V) will enable us to see whether a structure is active, and to what extent.

III – Present life experiences (from now back to the moment of conception):

As we go over some childhood circumstances that are specifically linked to each structure, we will bear in mind that their impact is due not so much to the circumstances themselves but to the emotional charge from past lives with which these present conditions will resonate, not to mention the individual's level of evolution.

On the other hand, the soul is consistent in its intention. If, for example, there are memories of deprivation or abandonment which need to be healed, there is a good chance that such situations will occur during the first few years of life. This is why we find some fairly typical childhood conditions related to each structure.

IV – The basic defence system related to the structure

Each type of non-integrated experience (as described in points II and III in relation to each structure) leads to the development of a specific defence system, which is the source of the characteristic daily behaviour patterns of each structure.

V – The automatic behaviours that are typical to the structure in everyday life (making it possible to detect whether or not it is active):

1—General attitude towards life

When our consciousness is locked into a particular structure, all our choices, preferences, aversions, decisions, from the minor ones to the most important ones, are dictated by the defence system rather than by the reality of the present moment. Generally speaking, we are not aware of this, and we assume that "this is the way we are." On the other hand, when our consciousness begins to awaken, we begin to ask ourselves why we react in this manner, and whether there might be a different way of responding to life, one that would yield more harmony and fulfilment in our lives.

2—Relationships

Knowing these structures will allow us to better understand the way we act in our relationships, and also to better understand others. This gives us precious tools with which to harmonise our relationships.

3—Sexuality

Sexual activity is an important part of relationships. When we are hung up by some structure, this automatically and powerfully conditions our sexuality, which then becomes a source of much pain and many difficulties, instead of a source of joy, sharing and freedom.

4—The physical body:

a. Body shape

The shape of our physical body in any given incarnation is affected by our defence systems.[5] So each structure will be associated with a typical body style, with more or less significant nuances stemming from other structures.

b. Health

Each defence system, which corresponds to a specific form of energy block, will tend to generate specific forms of illness.

c. Automatic choices in the way we dress

When the structure is active, all of our choices, whether major or minor in significance, are conditioned by it, against our better judgement or any kind of objectivity. It is interesting to note, for example, how we choose our clothes.

5—Energy profiles

Each structure results in a particular energetic profile for each person. Also it is interesting to note how we manipulate energy in our interactions with others. This is done unconsciously, of course, but it is quite active nevertheless.

6—Dealing with money and the material world

Each structure has its own particular way of dealing with the material world. Many difficulties we have in mastering this reality will disappear when we engage in appropriate deprogramming work.

7—Dealing with power

This is one of the most constricting of all destructive dynamics. As we observe how each untransformed structure uses power, we can see how the ego undermines the power of the soul and manipulates others. We can also see how the power of the soul can be recovered, for the greater good of all, once transformation has been achieved

8—Work

All the different structures, of course, can be identified in all types of jobs. Yet when we choose a professional occupation, our dominant structure will tend to push us towards an activity that corresponds to our defence system. The job itself is not the issue; whatever it may be, it serves a useful purpose in our society. It can be very liberating to become aware of these dynamics in relation to our work and career choices.

9—Service

Service is a direct manifestation of the will of the soul. Each structure has its own way of blocking or rechannelling this will for its own purposes.

10—The pitfalls of spiritual seeking

Just because we become involved in a process of spiritual work or inner inquiry, does not mean that we are rid of our structures, not by a long shot. As in other areas of human experience, unless we remain vigilant, a spiritual quest can easily be reclaimed by the ego, which then uses this quest to strengthen its defence systems instead of dismantling them.

Indeed the ego is not interested in any genuine spiritual quest that would erode its prerogatives. As the presence of the soul drives us nevertheless in that direction, the ego will do everything it can to divert the process to its own advantage, unless it manages to block it altogether. Many people, who think of themselves as being very "tuned in" spiritually, are actually just reinforcing more or less subtly the mechanisms of their personality. Others, on the other hand, though they may not profess any spiritual allegiance or pretension, are actually much closer to manifesting their soul, i.e. genuine spirituality. The inner journey is full of pitfalls, some obvious, some subtle, and we shall see that each structure has its own way of reclaiming the process of inner inquiry for its own purposes. Though one may be sincere at the outset, the ego will soon reveal itself with its arsenal of defence systems, which will be all the more persistent as the individual, under pressure from the soul, passionately seeks to shed all manner of limitations.[6] This is why knowing these structures can be a great help to making our spiritual inquiry more genuine, closer to the truth, and more effective, no matter what teaching, method, or path we choose to use.

11—Tasks involved and practical suggestions for transformation

Each structure involves a specific kind of work to do, and it is helpful to become clearly aware of it. It is a fact that any truly liberating work must involve unravelling the memories and the energy blocks built up in the past. A specific approach applied to the level of the unconscious, and enlisting the forces of the soul, is therefore required. I shall introduce certain aspects of this work later in this book.

However, at this stage, I will make certain practical suggestions that will prove helpful in our daily existence to begin to consciously derail the mechanisms of the structure. The mere fact of being able to take a step back and witness our own structures at work will make it possible for us to harmonise our daily lives to a great extent, to lighten our relationships, and to resolve many difficulties.

VI – The structure transformed

As we evolve towards higher levels of awareness, our defence systems soften, emotional charges are dissipated, and our structures become more supple. These structures, which were so constricting, become more and more imbued with the qualities nurtured by a rich treasury of past experiences, leading to wisdom, knowledge, mastery, and love. The ego then becomes a vehicle of expression for the qualities of the soul, which was the goal in the first place. This is how human beings evolve.[7]

An individual who has reached this point of transformation of his/her structure will then naturally behave in very different, often opposite ways from the automatic behaviours generated by previously rigid inner mechanisms. There is no longer any need for moralising, preaching, persuading, prompting or imposing one's will on others. Willpower, on the other hand, is a very important asset in order to accomplish the work involved in ego release, whether it is through some specific approach or through life's ups and downs. Yet once the process of liberation has been achieved, the energy of the soul is naturally, effortlessly, simply and powerfully expressed. These structures, therefore, are not something to be annihilated; all we need to do is to recognise and transform them.

VII- Summary outline of the characteristic features of the structure

A concise outline will summarise the main points covered.

2-4 The Five Main Character Structures

We will use Wilhelm Reich's terminology to identify the different types of structures. Reich was a practising psychiatrist, and therefore used terms that have a psychiatric resonance. In such a context, these terms imply some form of imbalance leading to illness, which is not what our study is about. While Reich broadened their meaning to give them a more therapeutic focus, we will use them in an even broader sense.

We will describe how a "normal" human being functions, i.e. one who manages to function more or less adequately in today's society. But functioning does not mean being fulfilled, serene, happy and in charge of one's life. For this reason, this is intended for people who have realised that conventional functioning is not enough, and who are looking for a higher level of fulfilment, a more profound experience of life—something more than material satisfaction or mere adjustment to ordinary living.[8]

We will use certain abbreviations (for example "schizo", instead of schizoid) to underscore the fact that this is a different reality from the meaning attached to such terms in conventional psychiatry or therapy, and different also from certain definitions given by Reich himself.

In fact, the link is still there. Unconscious structures are the same for all human beings. But some people have a very weak ego and must contend with a highly charged unconscious. For these people, depending on their state, therapy or psychiatry is a useful approach to simply stem the flow of the unconscious and allow "normal" functioning in an ordinary setting.

Others have a personality that is already relatively well integrated, stable and balanced. The unconscious, in this case, is relatively under control, though it still limits their freedom to be fully themselves, as well as their capacity for contribution. These are the people we are addressing, people who want to liberate themselves from the ordinary world of lower consciousness, in order to live in the extraordinary world of higher consciousness.

As we shall see, the behaviours described are quite familiar, as they are exhibited by perfectly "respectable", sometimes spiritually advanced people. We shall therefore ignore psychiatric or therapeutic definitions, and redefine each structure specifically, in the light of what we have discussed regarding the way the lower mind functions and the process of evolution in general.

The five major structures we will be looking at are the following:

STRUCTURE	EMOTIONAL CHARGE	DEFENCE SYSTEM
Schizo	Fear	Escape from reality
Oral	Deprivation and abandonment	Stuffing, dependence
Masochist	Powerlessness	Victim, submission, rebellion
Psychopath	Power and betrayal	Manipulation, performance, image
Rigid	Insensitivity	Control, domination

• Some final general comments
Caution: It is important to avoid identifying ourselves or others with the structures which will be described in the following pages.

These structures are about our instrument, the ego, for which we are responsible, **but they are not our true being**. In fact we "are" the structure only to the extent that we identify with our ego. But we must remind ourselves that **what we are, in essence, is our Self which is perfect**, and that it is only our instrument that, for the moment, remains constrained within rigid structures.

It is very useful, on the other hand, to get to know these structures well, for this will help us to gain a better understanding and a higher level of mastery of our instrument, knowing that we carry all of these structures within ourselves to varying degrees.

We have structures, but we are not these structures.

We will no doubt recognise ourselves, as well as many of the people around us, in the upcoming descriptions. Therefore, we should approach this study in a state of serenity and compassion for all the human suffering that is embedded in these unintelligent, inharmonious and destructive behaviours. Each of us needs love and understanding to heal the wounds of the past. May this knowledge provide us with an even deeper understanding of our inner reality, which will allow us to see others, as well as ourselves, as travellers on a path that leads eventually to the full expression of our inner perfection.

For the sake of simplifying our presentation, we will refer to the various behaviours directly by naming the structure under study, for example: "Orals behave in such a way." This does not mean that any individual is this structure. What this shortcut actually means is: "The part of the ego that is caught up in the oral structure will generate such behaviour." Or: "When we are stuck in the oral structure, we behave in such a way."

We will most often use the masculine gender, again for the sake of simplicity, though clearly these structures concern both sexes. In this regard, though there may be structures that are culturally more developed among men or among women, it is interesting to note that the fundamental traits of each of them are equally applicable to both sexes. In general it will not be necessary to make distinctions. At the level of our traumas, we all share the same history, and we are all in the same boat.

— · — · — · — · — · — · — · — · — · —

[1] Among the better known, let us mention: Lowen in Bioenergetics, John Pierrakos in Core Energetics, Barbara Ann Brennan, internationally known for her activities in the area of working with energy, and for her high quality teaching (Healing Through the Human Energy Field), etc.

[2] Indeed, Reich's approach focuses on experiences having to do with intra-uterine life, birth, and early childhood, and does not include the more general concept of the soul's mastery over ego. I have broadened this approach in order to get a more comprehensive view of the subject. His theories, however interesting they may be, are not the substance of this study.

[3] Pychoanalysis, psychosynthesis, transpersonal psychology, astrology, numerology, esoteric psychology, etc.

[4] Each defence system can be considered as a form of blocked energy. When it is unravelled, it does not just disappear. It unleashes the bottled up energy contained there, and that now becomes available to allow us to live life more fully.

[5] Indeed our physical form is moulded around our etheric body, and all our memories are energetically imprinted on our etheric body, which has a direct link to the mental body wherein these memories are stored.

[6] In fact, recognising and mastering our ego mechanisms is the foundation of any genuine spiritual quest.

[7] We realize that evolution is not a linear process resulting from rational learning, but rather a process of successive approximations. A "traumatizing" experience leads to the development of a defence system which, in the immediate sense, allows the individual to survive. This rigid system thus has some momentary usefulness, but it is nevertheless constricting, and it often generates very destructive behaviours. As time goes by and we experience life through this system, our personality matures through pain as well as joy, and the system becomes more supple; the emotional charges are dissipated through realizations fostered by lessons we learn in the school of life, a learning process that we can eventually accelerate through conscious and deliberate inner work.

[8] We are therefore a long way from psychiatry, and beyond the scope of conventional therapy. Though the information presented here can be very useful in therapeutic terms, as what is presently referred to as therapy covers very different levels. Some very open "therapeutic" techniques act as a great support for spiritual growth. In fact, in certain cases, it becomes rather difficult to distinguish an advanced therapeutic process from spiritual work.

chapter 3

The SCHIZOID Structure:
DENIAL OF INCARNATION
"I don't belong here"

A tree that has no roots cannot bear fruit.
—*African proverb*

3-1 Stories

As far as anyone can remember, Joe has always had his head in the clouds, dreaming and thinking of all kinds of things. He was rather shy and withdrawn as a young child, and did not play with other children. He would invent his own games and would tell himself stories. He found the people around him rather dull-witted and, more importantly, not very sensitive. He liked being alone, but was terribly afraid of the dark. When evening came, he would go home, and through the night he would live in fear of ghosts coming to get him. As a teenager, he pretended to take part in what his peers viewed as entertainment, but never took great pleasure in this. Girls frightened him, and he would stay away from them as much as possible. On the other hand, the rebellious mindset against the outside world that he found in many of his peers was attractive to him, though in him this rebellion took a rather passive and inert form, as he would turn down most of the activities offered to him, whether they came from his parents or from school. Even when he went out with friends, he would remain one step removed in his dream world, watching others get excited without the slightest inclination to follow suit. He would write a lot of poems, only to discard them afterwards. His thoughts often turned to the subject of death. As an adult, he never managed to choose a career, as nothing really interested him, other than certain artistic activities. In a pinch, he might have gone into computers, as the intellectual process involved was attractive to him. He ended up with a combination of both, studying computer graphics. He thus managed to earn a meagre living through occasional contracts. He was somewhat talented, but his energy quickly dissipated, and he became tired and lost interest in his projects the minute they required interactions with people. He often judged society, and the world at large, in rather negative terms.

Joe made a few attempts at getting involved in a love relationship. This was no easy thing for him, as he found women demanding and tiresome. They always wanted him to be present, to talk and to communicate, which was not really his thing. Being in a relationship was not one of his priorities, and rather than him going after women, what usually happened was that some woman picked him up (since he looked like a nice guy).

He would rather live in his dream world and his fantasies. In particular, he spent several years setting up plans to create a rather unique centre for contemporary arts, but nothing ever came of them. When the time came for action, there were always all kinds of good reasons not to make any concrete move. He drafted a number of different projects, some small, some grand in scale, though none were ever completed. Though he occasionally made a few concrete moves, if the project didn't come together easily, his motivation quickly waned, and he ended up slacking off and eventually dropped the project altogether, with the excuse that people are stupid, that they are just not ready for his brand of brilliance, and that life in this world is far too complicated and ultimately uninteresting.

Joe eventually managed to get married, without really trying. He used the marriage to leave most of the material responsibilities in the hands of his wife, as he continued to dream and to talk about his projects. Since he was incapable of generating a stable income, his wife shouldered the burden of their financial survival.

His ethereal attitude, often bordering on irresponsibility, was often very frustrating to the people around him, which didn't make his life any easier. He had little interest in family gatherings, group activities, or social events. Whenever he ended up with relatives or friends (mostly his wife's), he either took no part in the conversation and remained lost in thought, or he launched into long philosophical and highly intellectual discussions, which some found impressive for a while, but which invariably ended up boring everyone.

All of these behaviours, and others like them, make Joe's life profoundly unsatisfying, and he can't figure out why. He thinks life is a bitch, and that makes him want to withdraw even more, to further cut himself off from reality. He feels hounded by a pervasive state of unrest, sometimes to the point of anxiety, without really knowing why. This will go on until he falls into deep depression, or until his wife leaves him, or until some other major upset turns his life upside down, which will perhaps allow him to wake up and begin to realise that there may be another way of approaching life, one that might be more satisfying.

◆   ◆   ◆

Janet was very subdued as a child. She was a nice little girl who played alone, was very afraid of her father, and would vanish into the woodwork whenever he raised his voice. She was very timid and fearful of knives, mice, other children, the neighbour's horses, and her grandmother. During her teenage years, she was always in a dream. She went unnoticed, as if she didn't exist. She would be influenced this way and that by her peers, and behaved somewhat like Joe with his friends. She was, of course, very wary of boys. Light and delicate as a feather, she loved flowers, birds, and songs. As an adult, she finally found a husband (or rather a husband finally found her). Her health is very fragile, and her mother is often called upon to take care of the children. Her husband rules the household, and she has no problem following his lead, as long as he relieves her of all material concerns and doesn't ask her to make any decisions. She takes great interest in spiritual books, which her husband doesn't understand in the least. She takes courses in order to learn how to make contact with angels. She is very afraid to go out on her own, and would rather stay home than work at some outside job. While she was relatively close to her children when they were young, her mother, with her authoritarian disposition, was the one to look after material things; Janet finds the bond with her children getting more and more tenuous as they grow older. Yet this is of no great concern to her, as she can easily find refuge in her readings and her dreams. She has no idea that her husband is cheating on her. In any case, that would hardly upset her, as she feels very distant from him and has no interest in getting any closer than necessary. If he gets angry, she says nothing and withdraws into her dreams or her books. He often asks her where she is, to which she rather distractedly replies: "Why here of course!" But this is far from certain. Her "angels" have told her that she is a very advanced being of light, that people just cannot understand her, and that she is better off creating a separate world for herself. Thus Janet floats through life, until the day when perhaps she will be confronted with a challenge that will require genuine involvement on her part, where she will have to be fully present (illness, financial crisis, serious family problems, etc.). This will perhaps be a (painful) opportunity for her to realise that she is alive on this earth, and that there may be something for her to do on this lowly plane.

These two examples bring to light some of the characteristics of this first structure: low interest in integrating the physical world, reluctance to take part in it, withdrawal into a world of dreams or intellectual activity, little concrete action, very few relationships. When one is caught in the schizoid structure, **one is simply not there.**

Joe and Janet have good reason to behave in this manner. Though they may sometimes make an effort to get more involved, often at the request of the people around them, it is as if some powerful inner force prevents them from doing so. Something drains away their energy, dissolves their interest in what goes on in this world, and constantly nurtures an undercurrent of anxiety. The reasons for this type of behaviour, which produce very little satisfaction and much frustration for the individual concerned and for the people around him, are lodged at the level of the unconscious, which carries very particular kind of memories.

3-2 Past life experiences at the root of the schizoid structure

Generally speaking, this structure does not stem directly from early childhood circumstances. As we will see, such experiences only serve to resonate with more powerful experiences going back to past lives. I have observed many people who had a relatively normal childhood, without any major physical or psychological trauma, and yet were evidently caught in this structure.

The basic trauma stemming from past lives

The traumatic, i.e. unintegrated experience at the root of the schizoid structure is founded on situations that are felt as very painful and terrifying, with **great**

suffering in the physical body: these are experiences that the personality involved at the time was unable to integrate. These generally take the form of torture, physical violence, and all manner of abuse, which translated into tremendous bodily pain. Of course the individual does not recall such memories consciously, as this would be far too intense. But the unconscious remembers very clearly and builds its defence systems on the basis of such experiences, according to the principles described in Chapter 4 of *Free Your True Self 2* (how active memories come into being).

Because of these physical aggressions, the lower mind, burdened as it is with a heavy emotional charge, has registered the fact that living in a physical body involves the risk of enduring horrendous suffering, to the point of losing one's mind. For example, one may have gone through an experience where one was totally powerless in the face of physical pain, with a sense of imminent and final annihilation; the situation generated intense fear and death was welcomed as an end to the pain.

As a result of such unintegrated traumatic experiences, the individual has come to hate the physical world, and to conceive a deep wish never to come back to this plane of existence because it hurts too much. The memories carried by the mind when it put together the materials for a new incarnation were loaded with information to the effect that the physical world is definitely a harsh place filled with tremendous pain and horror, a place one must avoid getting mixed up with at all cost. **According to these memories, incarnating is the worst thing that can happen to a being.**

This reluctance to incarnate comes with a deep **fear**, an almost cosmic fear which has deeply embedded itself in the very core of one's cells, for while undergoing physical suffering and torture, the entire body was placed on red alert by one's survival instinct. This intense pain may have lasted hours, weeks, months, or even years, and often ended in violent death. The ego had time to build very strong cellular memories in relation to the horror of being bound to a physical body, ready to be reactivated in subsequent incarnations, following the dynamics described in Chapter 3 of *Free Your True Self 2*.

The schizoid defence system is partly responsible for the first type of personality/behaviour described in Chapter 2 of *Free Your True Self 2*, i.e. the one dominated by **fear**.

Such circumstances do not in any way affect the Self, which chooses the time to "go back down" to the physical plane once again in order to recreate its instrument in a new incarnation for further experiences. Yet as a result of the dynamics described earlier, when the personality is being formed and the necessary materials are being gathered from the three worlds for this new lifetime, the mental/emotional blocks are reinstalled so that they can be worked on. Reluctance to live in the physical world is thus inserted into this personality. The energy of the Self is stronger of course, and its consent to the process of reincarnation will prevail. But the new ego, on the other hand, will have a very strong resistance to any kind of participation in this world, and this resistance will be fuelled by a sort of deep, quasi-constant existential angst, for which the individual will have no real explanation. In fact, the individual will often be unaware of this angst, for his reluctance to take part in the physical world goes hand in hand with a **reluctance to feel**. Yet it remains very active in the unconscious, generating a great deal of stress, as well as physical and psychological ailments which stem from a deep-seated fear of living.

This evening, Ann decided to go to the movie theatre to see the latest version of Robin Hood. She is in great spirits and everything is fine. The film begins, and as the images unfold before her eyes, Ann suddenly feels terrible. She has trouble breathing and, though the film is captivating, she just can't wait until it's over. Often she just has to close her eyes during scenes that really aren't that terrible, objectively speaking. As she leaves the movie theatre, she feels weird, as if floating just above the ground. When she gets to her car with the friend who had gone to the theatre with her, she asks her to drive, as she really does not feel well. She closes her eyes and her breathing begins to accelerate. She feels overcome with rising panic, and suddenly she sees the following story unfold on her mental screen, which she later shared with me:

"I saw myself as a woman in her forties. I lived in a house in the forest. I am a healer who works with herbal remedies. People from the neighbouring villages regularly come to see me for remedies to their ailments. I am quite knowledgeable in this subject, and I have a keen intuition. My ministrations bring genuine relief to those who come to me for help.

Mine is an active yet peaceful existence. Yet one day, two armed men come to my house. They enter without knocking and summon me to come with them immediately. When I ask why, they turn ugly and force me into a cart. I try to find out what is going on, but neither wants to talk. We travel this way for some time until we get to an imposing residence which I understand belongs to the archbishop of the area. They lock me into a small, dank room and leave me there for the rest of the day, bringing me a meagre pittance for supper. I am worried: what do they want with me? Then they come to get me and, having gone through several rooms, I am forced down a small, damp stairway. I arrive in a vaulted room where three men are seated behind a table, waiting for me. Without preamble, one of them tells me that I am accused of sorcery, that I cast evil spells on good people, and that I am possessed by the devil. I try to explain my craft, but I am not allowed to speak. They tell me that they will do what it takes to expel the demon from my body. I am then brought to a smaller adjoining room where I can see what are obviously instruments of torture. I am petrified with fear. My emphatic denials and supplications are of no avail, and they take off my clothes and begin to brush a fiery torch along the front of my body. The pain is unbearable. I don't understand, I feel I am going mad. These men talk to me, but I don't even understand what they are saying. How long this lasted, I have no idea, but it seems like a very very long time. Eventually I slip into unconsciousness, and die from the pain. As I leave my body, I can see that it is horribly burnt, especially in the area of my breasts, but I no longer feel anything. I am no longer in this body, and so much the better. I also see how cruel these men are, and I am horrified. I want to leave this world and never come back. I then move upward, towards higher energies calling me."

In her present life, Ann had a vague notion that she was caught in a schizoid structure. She was not aware of its source, but the spontaneous resurgence of this "story" allowed her to understand many of her actions and choices, as well as the limitations of her present life. The opportunity to contact the memory imprinted at that fateful moment motivated her to speed up her healing process.

Let us remember that it is not the story itself that matters in terms of the active force of the memory, but rather the emotional charge (in this case fear, or rather terror) that resulted in the memory becoming fixed in the memory of the computer. This depends on the individual, and the same story can resonate quite differently from one person to another depending on their different levels of evolution.

If we stop to consider human history with all its wars, its injustices, its tortures and its incidents of cruelty, it comes as no surprise that each of us, to a certain extent at least, carries memories within him of certain past life situations that have the potential to generate this kind of structure. In the course of my work, I have witnessed the emergence and defusing of memories related to all sorts of torture and physical abuse, either from a recent or a more distant past—slavery, wars, invasions by enemies who abuse conquered populations, torture (Inquisition, tyrannical political regimes, the horrors of Nazi concentration camps), etc. These memories are active only to the extent that the individual undergoing such abuses was not able to integrate them. Yet it must be acknowledged that it takes a very high level of evolution to be able to experience torture or intense physical pain while maintaining a state of inner calm and peace! Since most of us have yet to reach that stage, active memories of this type are numerous and, even though we may not have a predominant schizoid structure, in most cases some inner part of each of us remains under a constant state of tension. That part of us fears this world and its inhabitants. It will do whatever it can to defend and protect itself. Generally speaking, it is deeply fixed in the unconscious, and is all the more potent in limiting our daily actions and blocking the energy we need to live fully, mostly without our being aware of it.

3-3 Present life experiences which foster the recreation of a schizoid structure

From the moment of conception and throughout the early childhood stage, we feel very vulnerable in our little bodies, at the mercy of all those around us. This vulnerability generates a state of hypersensitivity to any physical aggression or threat (whether actual or perceived as such), which will foster the reactivation of memories such as we have just described. In the case of this structure, what kind of present life circumstances would it take to restimulate active memories stemming from past lives? Let us observe some of the more salient points. It must be noted that this is not intended as a theoretical or speculative presentation, but that it stems from my observations of experiences undergone by a vast number of people in the course of their work aimed at unburdening their unconscious.

Reich felt that this structure was essentially built when the child had been unwanted by his mother. This may be a reason, but it is not the cause. Rather it is one occasion among many to reactivate the memory. True, from the moment of conception, one feels that one's physical body is totally subjected to the will of one's mother, and one feels quite powerless and dependent on her for one's physical well being. One may then "choose" (be energetically attracted by) a mother who does not want this child, and would rather see him disappear soon after the birth. From the outset, this choice will reactivate the fear and the memory already recorded, to the effect that the physical world is a cruel environment characterised by the threat of physical annihilation.

Yet this perspective can be greatly expanded. We have observed that the mother's rejection in this lifetime is only one of the factors involved in the development of this structure, and it may not even be a prerequisite. The memories in which this structure is rooted, and which are imprinted in the body, usually stem from far more violent past life experiences, and they are ready to be reactivated by many other factors occurring at the intra-uterine stage, during delivery, and which can be reflected in all the conditions affecting the child's arrival in this world:

Intra-uterine life

The physical complications that can happen during this period can reactivate old memories. For example, if there is a problem with the placenta, and the infant suffers as a result, this can reactivate memories of pain or death by poisoning.

Amniocentesis, injections, etc., are experienced as physical or symbolic "aggressions" upon the uterus.

The mother's and father's negative thoughts towards the child are another significant influence. Many studies on foetal life have been conducted, and it is now a known fact that the foetus registers all of these vibrations and reacts to them.

Conditions affecting delivery

Difficulties arising during the baby's passage through the birth canal can reactivate memories of crushing, suffocation (avalanche, rock slide, cave-in, etc.) or life imprisonment in a narrow cell where the individual ends up dying.

Physical aggressions experienced during emergency delivery techniques (forceps, or other techniques) can reactivate various forms of physical abuse accompanied by feelings of powerlessness.

Even without necessarily considering any kind of resonance with past lives, Stanislav Grof, the American psychiatrist, conducted a detailed study of the different stages of childbirth and the traumas apparently linked to them[1]. Bernard Montaud has also explored this subject in some depth, and he offers a very interesting perspective on the event of childbirth. Knowing the history of humanity, one can very easily see resonances with past lives emerging from their descriptions.

Birth and the infant's first encounter with the physical world

Besides the natural physical difficulties that can arise during the process of childbirth itself, the birthing techniques used as standard practice in western hospitals until now have served as effective triggers for reactivating memories of physical aggression.[2]

Indeed, a newborn infant is hypersensitive in its tiny body which has never been touched. Under "conventional" childbirth procedures, it will be subjected to several forms of manipulation which it can easily interpret as painful assaults: bright lights, ordinary noise, differences in temperature between the mother's warm womb and the birthing room, all these are harrowing experiences for the newborn infant, whose senses of sight and hearing are assaulted from the outset.

Cutting the umbilical cord too soon, before it has stopped beating, gives the infant the impression that someone has removed its source of life.[3] As soon as it arrives into this world, the infant feels that people are trying to annihilate it: what a great start!

Then holding an infant up by its feet is a very painful practice whereby it may relive many traumatic experiences of torture and hanging. There is no smile on an infant in this position—rather there is panic, and a cry of pain. The parents and doctors are happy—it's alive! Meanwhile what the infant is inwardly experiencing and reprogramming in its unconscious is far less pleasant: fear, panic, and terror at being in a physical body.

Then come the drops in the eyes and nose (another very stressful practice which reactivates all kinds of facial assaults), and the wash-up. Not very pleasant, as a welcoming ceremony! Then the infant finds itself being bundled up and taken to its crib.

This kind of arrival into the world is ideal for reactivating traumas related to torture and bodily pain. The infant is physically alive, but inwardly petrified. Will it still want to live in this world, after such a welcome? The schizoid structure has every opportunity to take root: "I knew it, my physical body is going to suffer in this hell hole, the world is a dangerous place, and I'm going to do whatever it takes not to be here. **I am afraid.**"

This traumatic birth experience has been exposed for many years now. In the 1970s, Dr. Leboyer[4] pioneered an alternative way of bringing children into the world with more gentle birthing techniques, where any form of treatment that might be interpreted as physical violence by the infant is avoided as much as possible. Others, including Bernard Montaud and the people in his team, have produced essential data to further our understanding of the unique and profound process undergone at the time of birth. Indeed physical conditions are not the only factors influencing an infant's experience of the birthing process, as it is hypersensitive to the overall psychological environment.

> *By all accounts, the foetus appears to live in a very particular state of consciousness, with a very vast scope of perception. At each stage, it faces death while learning to choose life, as if a ruthless natural process of initiation were taking place within it. The infant coming into this world is a spiritual giant, a giant in terms of courage. Meanwhile, we think we are just dealing with a fragile little body, knowing nothing of its trials, of what it sees and knows about us. Indeed, birth is a grand and profoundly solitary ordeal, where the infant constantly seeks help, yet finally comes to the terrible realisation that the only thing humans are really concerned with is its physical health. The newborn infant then utters a formidable cry as it arrives into this world. It screams, "I am here, but you don't see me!" as we look elsewhere, at its weight, its feet, its hips. Such is the terrible ordeal of the "other" birth, which leads to perinatal trauma, with its weighty consequences on the development of the child's future personality.[5]*

Birth is a major experience shared by all human beings, and, for many reasons, it is a highly charged event. We shall review this point as we present the third structure, for birth is also an occasion for other types of memories to be reactivated.

Our purpose here is not to question the competence of doctors or nurses. They did their best. Their care, attention, and knowledge were essential to ensure our physical survival. For many decades, they were simply unaware of the psychic reality of an infant during the birth process, and of the dynamics involved in the development of the unconscious. As this knowledge is now becoming more and more widespread, things are changing very rapidly in this area. Indeed, although two or three generations have had to go through this type of birth, our awareness has evolved, and this is reflected in more humane birthing practices. Standard birth conditions are now more flexible and closer to the Leboyer method. Human beings are thus given more and more chances to experience gentleness and respect as they are ushered into this world, which can only foster their integration in life.

Whenever we focus on this reality, our unconscious is always reactivated to some extent, and there may be a tendency to dismiss all this with a shrug. Yet we must remember that each of us creates whatever appropriate conditions are required for the kind of learning that must take place. The fact that, for a few decades, birthing techniques have tended to reactivate certain specific types of active memories should not be cause for grief...quite the contrary, in fact. It was probably the right time for a great number of human beings to bring back these distant memories in order to be able to defuse them and heal the past. Everything is perfectly in place in the process of evolution.

Early childhood and on through another lifetime

Certainly other events may happen later on that will deepen the impact of those initial experiences. Yet our observation is that the schizoid structure is essentially reconstituted from the moment of conception until birth, unless the present lifetime brings new experiences of torture and major physical abuse. From the moment of birth, the die is cast and generally the structure is reconstituted if that is what was meant to be. In time, other structures may be added, bearing their own characteristics.

3.4 The Schizoid Structure's Defence System

During those non-integrated traumatic experiences, the personality became rigidly ensconced in a particular defence system in order to deal with the fear of being in a physical body. This system involves an aggregate of automatic responses which will kick in whenever a situation reactivates the mechanism. The mere fact of being physically in this world is a reactivating situation for this particular structure. In other words, from the moment the individual wakes up in the morning and is back on this lowly plane of existence, the memories are reactivated. The rejection of life and the fear are there, most often as unconscious motivators deeply embedded in the computer's operating system, along with an equally unconscious desire to flee, to retreat from this world as much as possible. The defence system, in this case, is withdrawal and various forms of escape.[6]

Thus we have the following mechanism at work:

> ✓ **The underlying fear** of the structure: fear of physical existence.
>
> ✓ **Emotional charge: fear, anguish, anxiety.**
>
> ✓ **Defence system: escape, withdrawal** in all possible forms.
>
> This defence system comes with an underlying automatic mental attitude, which can be summed up as a "statement".
>
> ✓ **Statement of this structure:**
>
>
>
> "I'M OUT OF HERE ! "
> "I hate and despise this world; I am too afraid, I don't want to live here,
> I want to be somewhere else, anywhere but not here;
> I want to return to the place where I won't run the risk of being hurt..."
>
>

When this mechanism is deeply embedded in a person's memories, how is this translated in terms of behaviour?

3-5 Typical Behaviours of the Schizoid Structure

1) General attitude towards life
• Withdrawal from the physical world, escape, absence

This structure's defence system is **escape** from anything that can bring the individual back to being of this world and remind him that he is caught in this incarnation. Besides this automatic response, there will be an energy block in order **not to feel** either body sensations or emotions, so as not to be conscious that we are in fact here.

The **general withdrawal mechanism** will condition a set of very specific behaviours. This is not a conscious attitude, of course, yet its effect is no less determining in that it will manifest itself in a variety of forms, beginning with **withdrawal of energy**. The moment one is called upon to participate, to reach out, to relate, to create something concrete, to play a role in this world, i.e. to be here now, an alarm signal is set off in the computer, and the unconscious switches off the energy flow. The individual is suddenly no longer motivated, unable to make a move, and just wants to leave. He becomes absent. The message from the unconscious, at that moment, is more or less the following: "Look out: I've been caught once before in this world and it ended up being an extremely painful experience; this is dangerous, I'm not going to stumble into that again, let's get out of here, let's keep running as much as possible."

In this mechanism, one is at the same time very angry at the world for not giving us any room to exist. Thus, besides the need for escape, there is often a dynamic involving separation and contempt: "You don't want to make room for me, so I will hate you and despise you." This statement will remain as an undercurrent of any relationship in which the individual is involved. This translates into an inability to love and to feel loved which can ruin a whole lifetime of potentially rich experiences.

The behaviours related to fear and separation, which are part of the ego characteristics described in Chapter 2 of *Free Your True Self 2*, generally stem from this structure. Depending on the individual and the baggage carried from the past, other structures may reinforce this dynamic.

There are many ways of not being there, and these are not necessarily all used by the same person:

[*Keep in mind that in order to facilitate my presentation, I will use such expressions as "schizos behave in such a way" in order to describe behaviours resulting from this structure's activity. This actually should be taken to mean, "When we are caught in this structure, we behave in such a way," and not as an identification of the person with this struc*ture. *The same goes for other structures.*]

• Mental activity

The unconscious tries as much as possible to cut off the energy flow to the physical body. This withdrawal of energy can take two forms: **dreamer schizos**, and **intellectual schizos** (both can cohabitate within the same person). This translates into two types of behaviour:

—either the entire personality is asleep: little or no physical activity, weak emotional potential, little in the way of mental activity, vague dreams, lots of sleep and lots of daydreaming;

—or all the energy is concentrated at the mental level. The individual is intellectually very active. He easily finds shelter in theories and philosophical ramblings, takes a keen interest in anything that has to do with ideas, but always in a totally abstract manner. This is where we find people who see themselves as profoundly inspired, and who think they have major revelations to bring to this world. But though they may be good talkers, they usually have a rather low level of energy and are relatively unconvincing. They listen to themselves speak since, in any case, relating to others would mean entering the world, which is of little interest to them. Their audience is usually other schizos who share this attitude which to them is non-confrontational. Everything happens in the mind.

• Refusal to get involved

Whether in a relationship, a job, or some kind of activity.

• Flight from conflict

In this structure, one never deals head-on with conflict situations. Instead, one seeks escape, in some form or another.

• Constant need to escape to some other place

Schizos are often habitual travellers, at least psychologically if not physically. They are perpetually dreaming of moving on. They try one place, one job, one project, then move on to another. They are generally quite unstable, always ready to leave the minute things get a little rough or when they are required to come out of their shell a little more.

• Withdrawal into pseudo-spirituality

Schizos are often found in so-called "spiritual" groups. This structure naturally leads to the appropriation of spiritual seeking as a justification for escapism or withdrawal in various areas of life.

• Favourite schizo hobbies

Reading (lots and lots of reading), movies (not theatre, which is too close to real life), handicraft, daydreaming, spiritual seeking and, generally speaking, anything that leans towards intellectual, solitary or non-involving activity.

2) Relationships: ABSENCE OF THE HEART

The characteristics of this structure will result in the following consequences in the context of personal relationships:

—Has a hard time relating; reduced communication, since the individual
lives "elsewhere", with his head in the clouds.

—Has a hard time getting involved.

—A schizo is generally a nice, gentle person, who doesn't make waves in
the context of relationships, since he wants to avoid any confrontation.
Eventually, if things get really rough, he will disappear either physically or in
terms of energy output (becoming more and more absent, lost in thought, in
dreaming up new projects, in a world of his own).

—Schizos are often passive and rather "yin" people, who lose themselves
in a relationship, leaning on the other person's identity to get the feeling that
they exist. As they do this, they lose any real sense of their own existence and
live in the illusion of a relationship. There is no conflict, but the other senses the emptiness he/she is faced with, and eventually tires of this perpetual
absence, even if the individual is very devoted and "nice". This eventually
leads to separation, and the schizo, in his avoidance of feeling, will generally
not make a scene. He will take refuge in his world of dreams and ideas, but
will feel little or nothing.

—Selfishness in the form of avoidance of responsibility: one disappears the
moment there is talk of commitment. Selfishness also in the form of
"absence" out of an unconscious avoidance of feeling that other people are
there, people with whom one might be called upon to share, or who might
sometimes need our attention.

—One projects emotional illusions (which are often idyllic at first) in order
not to have to face reality. This can even take the form of bouts of emotional
exhilaration, as a way to disconnect from reality. Everything, including the
significant other, is perceived as being inundated with light, everything is
incredibly beautiful. It will take a number of shocks for the individual to
come down from his cloud and face reality, particularly with regard to his significant other, with his/her all too human assets and limitations.

—Little or no courage; there is nothing to be gained by taking chances,
especially at the psychological level. Relating in a genuine way always involves
some risk for the ego, which the structure simply will not allow. So one simply glides above it all.

—One often hides behind one's partner, as a protective screen from the
outside world.

—One is out of touch with one's emotions, as one tries to avoid feeling:
one tends to escape the minute emotions come into the picture. At the same

time, one is very fragile when emotions do, in fact, surface, since mastery is somewhat lacking in this area, and one therefore feels very vulnerable.

—Pride: as he turns away from the world, the schizo feels very different and often superior with regard to others. This is a defence mechanism designed to allow him not to feel a part of this world.

3) Sexuality

The schizo is usually not very active sexually or, if he is, it is for selfish purposes, for personal transcendence. He uses orgasm and physical pleasure as a springboard to his private world, where he can escape reality.

4) The physical body
• Body shape

The physical body is often very tall and thin, with long legs and a lanky look. It seems as if the schizo, in his desire to leave this world as quickly as possible and return to the subtle worlds, will take a light and very elongated body, seemingly ready to leave the earth. One senses that the individual is somewhat unstable on his feet. Or one might find smaller but frail and light bodies.

• Health

This fear and this unconscious refusal to be here will translate into a variety of symptoms, specifically:

—Underlying anguish and anxiety, most often without any external reason, a basic anxiety towards life and a permanent state of stress. This can be the source of a number of health related problems.

—Depression, lack of energy, chronic fatigue, problems with concentration and memory: this makes sense since the defence system is itself based on a dynamic of withdrawal and escape. As the unconscious constantly withdraws energy, the individual becomes depressed, loses interest in living without knowing why. He wants to take pills or other substances in order to feel better, which, of course, only serves to cover up the real cause and weaken the physical body even more. Schizos are often attracted to drugs/medications that tend to propel them out of their everyday physical reality. A deep existential anxiety underscores all of these symptoms.

—Immune system deficiencies, as the unconscious refuses to fight, and this dynamic becomes reflected at the physical level.

—Blood circulation problems: I have noted that schizos often have cold hands and feet. This also makes sense, since the unconscious which controls energy output is very consistent in terms of its objective. The body's limbs are the instruments of manifestation: we do things with our hands, we move in the world with our feet. That is enough for the defence system to withdraw energy from these places. Low energy translates into slower blood flow, and thus cold hands and feet. We have observed a number of cases where people quickly and naturally regained warmth in their body extremities, once they were able to unravel this structure.

• Automatic choices in clothing

A somewhat casual appearance: looking good is not important since one is not really there. Along with this tendency, we might also come across a somewhat studied look, but with clothes of a rather unique or offbeat style. This is a way of letting others know that one is different, that one does not associate with common mortals.

• Keeping one's awareness out of the physical body as much as possible

The schizo will not be interested in taking care of his physical body specifically, unless this has to do with some theory or philosophy. In such cases, the individual easily becomes a fanatic, for example with regard to diet, as this apparent discipline does not actually stem from genuine attention to the needs of the body, but rather from an intellectual theory which may be more or less appropriate. For example, we might come across people who fast for prolonged periods of time when that is somewhat inappropriate in their case, or who go through extravagant cures without regard for the real needs of their bodies. This apparent attention to the body is, in fact, nothing more than a kind of unconscious assault on the body.

Except for such cases, a schizo tends to ignore his physical body, which he would often rather not have. Sports, or any other form of physical activity which might bring him back to this plane of existence, are avoided. Or the individual's rejection of physical reality may make him thoughtless to the point of recklessness. In such cases, the individual's inner disconnectedness and inability to feel will prevent him from having an accurate sense of proportion with regard to the physical laws of the material world. He may also look for thrills in order to recover some sense of his body, while at the same time harbouring an unconscious desire for a quick and final end to it all.

5) The energy aspect

Most of the energy is concentrated from the neck up. The lower chakras which are more closely linked to one's manifestation in the world, are rather inactive. Schizos generally have low levels of energy and are very quickly tired, no matter what they undertake.

When one is in the presence of a schizo, one feels a light, unobtrusive form of energy. This is not necessarily pleasant, as it is felt as a kind of absence that becomes draining over time.

6) Relating to the material world and money

Generally speaking, schizos tend to float above material concerns. They have a low level of mastery on the material plane, in whatever form, yet this does not bother them all that much. They will rarely be financially wealthy or, if they are, it will be thanks to their parents or someone in their immediate circle, a spouse perhaps or someone else, but certainly not as a result of their efforts. They can be very generous, but their generosity is somewhat irresponsible, stemming from an unwillingness to face material limitations. Or they can be very selfish and unaware of the needs of others around them. The unconscious systematically withdraws energy whenever circumstances call for wise and thoughtful action in the material world.

Schizos are easily influenced and manipulated as consumers, as they offer little resistance to a well trained salesperson. Since they take little interest in material things, they will tend to trust any so-called knowledgeable or apparently knowledgeable specialist, in order to avoid any material involvement.

This structure often generates contempt for the material world, not out of genuine detachment, but out of the individual's reluctance to get involved. In cases where this person is responsible for a family or business, he will inevitably be faced with a number of difficulties.

7) Relating to power

The schizo mechanism does not directly translate into a quest for power over people and things, since it tends to make one disconnected from reality and reluctant to get involved in human relationships. This structure therefore tends to make a person **deny his own power** first of all, for having power means being able to create concrete things in this world, to act alone and with others, to get involved and to manifest one's intent in some way. The unconscious fear is too great, so that the individual stays aloof from everything and everyone. To avoid the risk of confronting life's difficulties, a schizo refuses to take charge of his own power.

When faced with other people's power, real or imagined, whether or not it is authoritarian in nature, a schizo will simply slip away. He vanishes physically or psychologically, or he pretends to submit while disconnecting himself from the situation, by escaping or taking refuge in an attitude of contempt.

In a group situation, a schizoid structure will be felt as a dead weight that resists creation and concrete manifestation, often with nicely laid out theories or explanations that justify non-action. In this sense, he resists other people's creative power.

Obviously, under such conditions, a schizo will greatly limit his own power, but he doesn't care.

8) Work

A schizo will rarely be found holding a stable, conventional job, unless it happens to be a place where he is left alone to dream and make himself scarce. He will rarely be involved in a long-term occupation.

He lacks practical sense. He may have some fine perceptions of the world, or he may design and map out grand projects, often with laudable spiritual or humanitarian goals, but these will tend to be completely unrealistic. The question of realism is not even raised, as he unconsciously has no intention of actually completing anything. In his denial of the physical world, he refuses to consider its limitations. He therefore most often meets with failure, and then blames the world for these failures (other people are just not smart enough, not ready to grasp his great ideas!). This just makes him even more ensconced in his structure: he just does not fit into this world that was not meant for him.

Schizos are often found looking for "work". But they rarely succeed in their endeavours. Doors keep closing one after the other, and they don't understand why. The trouble they have in "succeeding" stems from their unconscious attitude of withdrawal. They are not inwardly very strong, and are easily manipulated by structures of a psychopathic or rigid nature, as will be examined further on, who will get them into all sorts of wild schemes for concrete projects that eventually turn out to be dead ends.

As far as work is concerned, schizos will tend to operate on their own as much as possible. They will initiate their own projects, which will later fizz out. They will often be observed going from one project to another, one failure to another, without being able to learn the lesson embedded in these failures, unless they manage to use them as springboards for their own awakening.

A schizo will often be found in various intellectual, artistic, or "spiritual" professions, where he can function without being involved and without relating to others. Many schizos work with computers, a good way to avoid human reality and to function strictly on a mental level without the need to feel anything.

He will feel good whenever involved in artistic activities, where he will tend to be somewhat brilliant, using art not as an expression of the soul, but as a means of escape. He will think of himself as a highly inspired genius, despising this lowly world that cannot give him the recognition he deserves.

He will also be found in a number of New Age trades that give a person a sense of working with "new energies" based on "spiritual" philosophies and beliefs. For example, they will often be found working as therapists using all kinds of approaches: healing through angels, crystals, sound, light, mantras, divine energy, clairvoyance, channelling, etc. Such activities may be quite valuable in themselves, but the structure often appropriates them to reinforce the individual's disconnectedness from reality, rather than lead to a genuine form of concrete mastery.

Trades or activities where schizos will often be found[7]: artists (especially painters and musicians), computer programmers, philosophers, "spiritual" instructors and therapists, various New Age activities, offbeat and unstable occupations (requiring no involvement).

9) Service

Serving requires a person to be there and to get involved, something this structure does not allow. So there is very little interest in concrete service activities. On the other hand, once this structure has been transformed, this soft and over-accommodating attitude will develop into remarkable qualities of compassion, service and dedication. But before one can dedicate oneself to any endeavour, one must first of all exist. As long as one has not had the courage to define one's own existence, one can only give very little, as one tries to survive and relies on others instead of being a creative source.

10) Pitfalls in spiritual seeking

Schizos often take refuge in spirituality, not to do any genuine work of inner transformation, but as a justification for leaving the material world and focusing on other worlds which, according to their memories, are more hospitable than this one. They can be passionate meditators (while meditating, one is not of this world, and one is unlikely to be disturbed by anyone), and ardent consumers of all kinds of spiritual teachings, as they cut themselves off from the real world and isolate themselves in ideals and visions that allow them to disconnect from everyday reality. Clearly, the value of meditation and spiritual teachings is not in question here, as these are excellent when they are used in order to bring about a greater manifestation of the soul in the world, rather than as a means of escape.

Schizos tend to choose paths requiring relatively little discipline (unless this structure is combined with the fifth [rigid] structure). As they are very attracted to anything that has to do with "subtle" energies, they will seek to contact spiritual guides, angels, and the "energies", which are most often nothing more than astral illusions. They will themselves easily develop so-called lower psychic powers (clairvoyance, clairaudience). They may be involved in "channelling", receive a multitude of messages from spiritual worlds which, in most cases, are merely easy connections to the astral plane and are only valuable, at best, as generalities. "Spiritual group" gatherings are appealing to them to the extent that everyone involved nurtures the same illusions.

Here again, the activities themselves are not in question. It is possible for us to make contact with subtle worlds and to receive information in a serious and meaningful manner. But this cannot occur without a high degree of development on the level of our intelligence and discrimination, as well as our capacity to remain truly centred and grounded.

Schizos who are involved in a spiritual process will often be interested in bookish teachings of all persuasions. Any theory on which they can philosophise, from the most serious to the most hare-brained, will do just fine as long as it doesn't involve any form of concrete manifestation.

This structure, which is often very much into spirituality, will tend to appropriate genuine teachings and turn them into justifications for escapism. For instance, many teachings point to the necessity for detachment with regard to the material world, which is totally valid. But this will be appropriated by the schizoid structure to justify its contempt and denial of this world, to avoid responsibility and to withdraw from it.

In the same way, this sort of individual will justify his refusal to relate, to act and to build, i.e. his refusal to use his power to fully manifest himself, with beautiful spiritual theories on desirelessness and on how unreal this world is. In such cases, this does not stem from genuine detachment at all, but from the fear of fully experiencing his humanness. His spiritual theories will also allow him to justify his spectacular failures in the world of concrete manifestation, whether they have to do with work-related projects or with relationships.

11) Some practical suggestions and tasks leading to transformation

The transformation required of a schizo is to **free himself from his deep-seated fear and denial of the physical world, and to fully and joyfully allow himself to play in the world in a well-grounded way**. This obviously cannot be done through an intellectual process, and liberation will require deep inner work at the level of the memories. On the other hand, if we can recognise ourselves in this structure, we can begin to work on it consciously on a daily basis, through certain choices and activities, for example:

—act on a project and bring it to completion, however modest it might be

—continue to dream, but develop concrete objectives

—dare to manifest ourselves concretely and place ourselves in circumstances that will bring us back to the practical reality of this world

—practice perseverance and willpower

—learn to recognise precise moments when we are tempted to flee, and the means we use to do this; become aware of this mechanism

—get involved in activities that require relating to others (for example: volunteer groups, theatre, team sports)

—learn to manage our time

—take responsibilities and meet them efficiently and consciously

—dare to confront our fear and overcome it, in order to act and to communicate

—strive to genuinely communicate with others, both through self-expression and through active listening

—draw inspiration from examples of action and courage

—get into physical activities: gardening, cooking, dancing, sports, martial arts, acrobatics, anything that requires discipline, involvement and presence, with others whenever possible adopt a large dog

3-6 The Schizoid Structure Transformed

When this structure is defused, the defence system disappears, and its inherent qualities come to the surface. Through inner work focused on deactivating fear and denial of the world, it becomes possible for the personality to integrate all past experiences which are linked to these memories. When that happens, the energy that was blocked now becomes available to carry out the will of the Self. This energy is not neutral: it is endowed with all the colours of past experiences. This gives a particular tone to the personality, and some very interesting qualities. The once limiting aspects are now transformed into assets.

This structure gives a person **a natural ability to contact subtle worlds**, a heightened sensitivity and receptivity to high-level energies. When transformed, i.e. when the individual is totally present in this world, this contact with other dimensions of consciousness can be used to create a genuine link between the physical world and worlds of higher consciousness.

This can take different forms such as art, for example. Through "inspiration", great artists are able to contact very high planes of beauty, which they then manifest on the physical plane. This can also take the form of humanitarian projects, successful ones at that, through which the individual will use concrete accomplishments to ground his love and compassion for mankind. Or it can happen through spiritual teachings or some activities related to subtle worlds, only now these will be combined with solid intelligence, real knowledge, objectivity and discrimination: head in the clouds but feet firmly on the ground. It can take the form of scientific discoveries, which will have a genuine impact in terms of the advancement of science, instead of being gratuitous mental constructs. Indeed, great scientists are attuned to very high levels of the universal mind, which is where their discoveries spring from. This can happen in a number of ways.

One does not have to have a transformed schizoid structure in order to be a great artist or scientist. All that can be said is that this experience, once integrated, can open the door to personal development in this direction. All the other wealth of knowledge and experience accumulated by the soul in the course of its history can now be manifested in the world, as the individual is now willing to be here, to play the game of life and to make a contribution.

Other features of a transformed schizoid structure

Once liberated from the fear underscoring this particular defence system, the individual will naturally live with a great sense of lightness. He becomes a very pleasant, funny, and most of all highly creative person. He will be capable of a great deal of spontaneous **originality**, of astonishing **creativity**, of uncommon **intuition**, of **light-hearted joy** much like a child's.

Knowing the benefits of elevated thinking, and having clearly experienced the tension between the spiritual forces of the Self and the fear stemming from the ego, the individual can use the vantage point of this transformed structure to easily understand, support and inspire others in their inner quest, and make it possible for them to avoid some of the major pitfalls of the spiritual path.

Detachment is easily attainable to a transformed schizo. This structure has had a tendency to resort to false detachment out of fear and a need to escape. When the traumatic memory is defused, what remains is a natural capacity for detachment, which can be used to create and to be free, without becoming unduly attached to any material thing or to any person. This quality makes it easier for the individual to stop identifying with his personality. He knows...he senses that he is not his ego, and this is very helpful knowledge on the way to manifesting the Self.

Another great quality of the soul, which is akin to detachment, is the quality of **impersonality**. Having experienced a tendency to deny his own existence, a schizo will find it easy, once transformation has occurred, to continue in this direction, this time with a totally accurate and objective sense of not attributing an excessive amount of importance to his own person. He finds it very easy to let go, to stop wanting to be right at any cost. This is not so easy for others, especially for the fourth and fifth (psychopathic and rigid) structures.

In the context of close relationships, such an individual will be very pleasant, and emotionally unburdened. He will be able to get involved without making a big deal out of it. He can easily see divinity and light in another person, and is able to give his partner a great deal of freedom. Rather than attachment, there is a great respect for the other person in terms of his/her own integrity and originality.

At work, he will obviously be a very creative person, while also being highly efficient. The individual will perhaps need a lot of freedom of movement to give free reign to his creativity, but he will also adapt very easily to various conditions.

As with any of the other structures, this liberation of the schizoid structure always eventually occurs, sooner or later. Part of the process will of course take place during the intervals between physical lifetimes, when a being continues to have experiences in the astral and mental planes, and then when the soul takes stock of the learning acquired. But the most important part of this process must take place during the individual's bodily existence, in order to bring this transformation down to the level of matter, especially in the case of the schizoid structure. Any self-transformation work that a person undertakes in this direction in a conscious and wilful manner brings with it a great sense of liberation and the ability to access a great deal of potential which would otherwise remain blocked for a long time to come.

Declaration of transformation

I am willing to live in this world. I bring to it my inner light.
I manifest my existence through willpower, perseverance and courage.
I dare to get involved and to create in a concrete way with others.

Contribution task

The greatest contribution that a transformed schizoid structure can make is to materialise all the beauty, wisdom and knowledge gleaned from subtle worlds through intuition, inspiration, and openness to new ideas and exceptional creativity.

3-7 The Schizoid Structure – Summary

• **Underlying fear of this structure:** fear of life, fear of involvement

• **Source experiences in the past:** great physical suffering

• **Emotional charge:** fear

• **Defence system:** withdrawal, escapism, absence, and separation

• **Declaration of the defence system:** "I'm out of here"

• **Needed work** (tasks required for the transformation of the personality): develop a willingness to be in this world, get involved, unabashedly play the game of life; ground oneself in earth energies; see the spiritual dimension of matter

• **Declaration of transformation:**

> I exist and I am safe
> in this world

• **Fundamental qualities of the soul to be recovered:**

> Security, exultation in one's existence
> in a physical body, concrete manifestation.

• **Qualities of the structure, once transformed: CREATIVITY, INTUITION,** openness to new things, genuine contact with subtle energies, joy, lightness of being, freedom, originality, ability to unabashedly play the game of life, light-hearted humour, natural respect for other people's space, detachment, impersonality, adaptability, uninhibited, light and joyful relationships.

• **Contribution task:**

> Concrete manifestation of the beauty and harmony
> of spiritual worlds in the physical world.

Bravo, all you schizos: you made it!

---

[1] Stanislav Grof, *The Adventure of Self-Discovery*.

[2] The "rebirth" theory places great emphasis on these conditions. They are indeed important, not necessarily as a primary cause, as they have often been presented, but rather as triggers for reactivation. The effectiveness of rebirth techniques is largely due to the fact that by liberating experiences undergone during birth, one simultaneously liberates a whole chain of past life experiences where physical aggression was involved, without necessarily being aware of it.

[3] This was common practice for years in conventional hospital procedures during childbirth, and this has produced a number of serious consequences (see Chapter 5). Yet nature works marvellously. All we have to do is wait 10 to 15 minutes for the umbilical cord to stop beating, and the infant feels neither pain nor any sense of separation. On the other hand, in our constantly hurried society, we do not take the time to respect such natural rhythms. In fact, everyone involved wants to get this birth over with as quickly as possible, as all stakeholders, doctors, nurses, parents, are unconsciously reactivated by this event according to their own birth experience, if they have not taken the time to go through the inner work involved in liberating the unconscious at this level (when we reach a generally higher state of awareness, this process of liberation will become part of the training program for obstetricians and nurses.)

[4] Quoted from a presentation to Bernard Montaud's book, *L' accompagnement de la naissance*, éd. Édit'as.

[5] This structure is often the source of the major challenge it is for some people to get up in the morning, and the fact that it takes them several hours (or a strong cup of coffee) to really be back in this world. Getting up, in effect, tends to reactivate the birth process. Indeed, as we sleep, our consciousness escapes to more subtle planes. As we wake up, it is drawn back into the physical body. The bed represents the mother's womb, where we were physically safe from the torments of this world and where we were still in contact with "other worlds". As far as the unconscious is concerned, getting out of bed is like being born again. It will therefore resist and withdraw its energy as much as possible. We have witnessed a great number of cases where people found themselves spontaneously filled with energy from the moment they wake up each morning, and ready to fully live each moment of the day, once they have defused this structure, even if only partly.

[6] Let us remember that the trade itself is not the issue, but rather what the individual chooses to do with his trade. Just because we may happen to be in one of these situations doesn't mean that we are necessarily schizos, and schizos can also be found in other occupations. We have simply noted that, notwithstanding other factors, these particular working conditions tend to be preferred by this structure, as this defence system tends to function better in such an environment. The more evolved a person becomes, the more he will manifest the qualities of this structure, and be able to create very beautiful things within his occupation.

chapter 4

The ORAL Structure
DEPRIVATION, LOSS, ABANDONMENT
"I can't have enough"

*He who drinks the water I have to give
shall never again be thirsty.*
—Jesus (John, 4)

4-1 Stories

Charles had a so-called "normal" childhood. His parents were nice folks who owned a small retailing business. Since they were very busy with their work, they didn't have much time to be with their two children, but this did not seem to be a problem. At the age of two, Charles had to stay in the hospital for one month to be treated for a malformation of the legs. He only has a vague and rather unpleasant recollection of this event. The nurses were kind to him, but he remembers how much he missed his mother. He often cried alone at night, wondering if she would come to visit him the next day. In fact, being very busy with her business and knowing that her son was in good hands, she only came to see him on Mondays, when the store was closed. On those occasions, she would bring him his favourite chocolate candies and cookies, but this fell far short of filling the awful emptiness he felt whenever she left. When the time came to return home, he was very glad, but his mother was still unavailable to take care of him, as the store kept her busy. For several months following his return, Charles cried almost every night. His mother did not understand why, since the operation had been a total success and Charles no longer felt any pain in his legs. Apart from this incident, his childhood seems to have unfolded normally.

These days, Charles works as a branch manager in a large chain of food stores. He likes his job, but he can't seem to find satisfaction in his life. First of all, he has a weight problem. His line of work provides easy access to all kinds of foods, which doesn't help when it comes to controlling his appetite. He has been toying with the idea of getting into some kind of sport in order to lose a few pounds, but his motivation is never strong enough to translate into action. Whenever he takes a vacation, he heads for the seaside, where life is good, where the food is plentiful, where first rate services can be counted on, and also where it is easy to meet beautiful women. "Club Med" resorts are right up his alley, since everything is provided on an all-you-can-take basis, and he knows he will lack for nothing.

He is very careful with his material possessions, and has many duplicates and tripli-
cates of certain items, just in case they become hard to find on the market. He has accu-
mulated an unbelievable number of objects, and his house is like a squirrel's hole filled
with supplies for decades of famine and deprivation. Even though he is materially very
well off, he is constantly on the lookout for any possible bargain. Having more for less is
a source of pride and joy. He loves to receive presents, though he seldom thinks of giving
any, or if he does, they are usually well below his means. He is very afraid of lacking in
anything, especially money, and this is a permanent source of stress for him.

His relationships never seem to work out very well. At 35, he lives alone. True, his girth
does not make him very attractive physically. Yet he loves women and has had several
relationships, but all his girlfriends have left him fairly quickly. He dreams of a relation-
ship where he could constantly cuddle up to his beloved, who would give him all the com-
fort and energy he needs. They would thus spend hours holding each other and tenderly
making love, and then sleep close together the whole night through. He feels that such a
nurturing relationship would make him the happiest man in the world. This ideal woman
would not only be sexually very attractive, but she would be faithful and always ready to
meet his needs, both emotional and sexual. But the women he meets don't seem to under-
stand his dreams of love and union. They complain of many things, especially his emo-
tional dependence and his constant demands. Each time, they become more and more
impatient and unpleasant, until finally they leave him. Charles still does not understand
why. He's a nice, intelligent, loving kind of guy, and doesn't see why he has been dropped
so often by the women who mattered most to him. Of course, some of them became
attached to him, but he soon found them too demanding and lost interest in them. Then
he would be the one to look elsewhere.

He compensates for these failures in his love life with intensive stuffing, with food, of
course, since this is his weakness, but also with shopping, travels, and overconsumption
at all levels. When loneliness drags him down, he eats chocolates: he knows this is not
going to help his weight problem, but he just can't help himself, since it seems to lift his
spirits and make him feel better, at least for a while. He is a passionate music lover, and
frequently upgrades his whole sound system to make sure he has the best. He doesn't part
with the old ones, though, in case he might need them some day. He also keeps records
that he hasn't listened to for years, for no good reason really. In certain areas, he spends
lavishly in a very emotional and irrational way, while in other areas, he can be surpris-
ingly thrifty.

These behaviours, which have a strong conditioning influence on Charles's life,
actually stem from a desperate effort to avoid a sense of deprivation that nothing
can assuage. Yet Charles had not had a particularly difficult childhood, apart from
his stay at the hospital. He had never undergone any real "traumatic" experience
at an early age. In his case, the experience of deprivation and abandonment was
imprinted in his memories long before his birth. These old memories, which were
reactivated simply as a result of a stay in a hospital, are what kept him in a constant state of insecurity and neediness.

This type of behaviour, which is common in our society, is not necessarily dysfunctional. Charles was able to earn a living and spend his money, and in our

society this is viewed as a sign of health. On the other hand, since he lived more or less unconsciously in a state of constant insecurity, expectation and neediness, any potential for clear and happy relationships, for beauty, for fulfilment, and for any deep satisfaction in life constantly eluded him.

Heather was one year old when her mother died. An aunt took her in and took good care of her for a while. But four years later, the aunt became very ill and had the child turned over to public services. Heather was then placed in a foster home. She felt very lonely. In addition, whenever she started to get used to a place or a family environment, she was moved to another place and she couldn't understand why. She ended up having a rather chaotic childhood, though the families that took her in had been good to her. She managed to study to become a psychotherapist, and this is the work she now does in a social service centre. She likes being in a helping relationship because she needs to be in contact with people. Yet she doesn't find this activity totally fulfilling. She often comes home feeling exhausted and dissatisfied. She would like to have a stable client base, with whom she could build interesting connections, but people just seem to stream through her office, and are gone before she knows it. Her husband is a good and loving man, yet she feels he doesn't give her all the affection she really needs. She has girlfriends, but they never seem to be available enough for her. She needs company so much. She is becoming more and more despondent, and beginning to lose weight. There's this great sense of emptiness in her life.

The lives led by Charles and Heather, their choices, their emotional reactions, and their physical and emotional "needs", are conditioned by a second type of structure, the oral structure. Certain elements in their present relatively normal lives have reactivated certain types of memories.

The oral structure stems from a defence system built as a result of an experience where certain vital physical or affective needs were not met. This created a **strong sense of deprivation, loss or abandonment** that the individual was not able to integrate. This defence system generates a permanent sense of **emptiness to be filled**, of being deprived of something essential for one's personal happiness. No matter what one does or receives, it is never enough to feel good. Fulfilment is unattainable in this structure.

4-2 Past life experiences at the root of the oral structure

Two types of "past life" experiences can deeply entrench the sense of deprivation in which this structure is rooted:

—On the one hand, physical deprivation of the most fundamental requirements for survival: famine, poverty, lack of water, unavailability of health care during illness, etc. These experiences may have lasted months, or even years, and have most often led to physical death. The deprivation was acutely felt and it had time to become deeply imprinted in the individual's unconscious and cellular memory.

—On the other hand, abandonment or loss occurring at a psychological level, with serious consequences for the rest of one's lifetime. This can take the form of physical abandonment, most often combined with a major affective loss, or psychological abandonment. If this leads to physical ailments, the experience will become imprinted even deeper into the memories.

Mark was brought up in a wealthy family. As an adult, he chose a career as an engineer because of the job security it would provide, though he really didn't need it since a regular income from family assets gave him a high level of financial security. In spite of that, he worried a great deal about the future. He would inwardly create a constant stream of catastrophic scenarios: job loss, illness, loss of financial investments, etc. His inner tension had become so strong that his health began to seriously deteriorate. At this point, he initiated a process of inner work. As he tried to find the source of his worrying, he realised that he was afraid to find himself in a materially deprived state to such a degree that it might prove deadly. This totally irrational fear led him to further inquiry, from which emerged the following "story", from deep in his unconscious: "Mark" sees himself in a city in the Middle East, around the tenth century. He is the son of a wealthy merchant, living in the lap of luxury. One day, however, there is news of an invasion by a hostile army. Indeed, the next day, the city comes under attack, and those who resist are massacred. Mark finds a hiding place in the cellar of his father's large house, and hears the screams of those who are being killed, especially those of family members. Then all is quiet, but he doesn't dare come out, preferring to remain in hiding until hunger sets in. He decides to go out at night to try to find something to eat, which is very dangerous, for if he should get caught, he would surely be killed. These are days of stress and anguish. Then one night he goes out, and when he returns, he finds that he can't go back in his hiding place, for two soldiers have apparently set up camp in front of the door to the cellar. Mark sees no other alternative but to leave the city and try to get to a village, some forty to fifty kilometres away, where family members who escaped the massacre have surely sought refuge. He knows that he will have to cross a desert, but he has no other choice. He manages to get a good supply of water, and sets off on his journey. He walks for several days, often having to make detours in order to avoid running into groups of horsemen. At one point, he realises that he is lost. He should have come upon the village a long time ago. He has run out of food, and his water supply is dwindling. He tries to stretch his rations, but exhaustion and lack of food soon reach an intolerable level. He continues to walk for hours, until the moment comes when there is no more water. No village in sight. Hunger and thirst overwhelm him, and he is unable to walk another step. There is nothing left but hopelessness and pain. Thus he dies in the desert.

Mark still carried within him the memory of that pain due to cruel deprivations acutely felt in his physical body. His present life was conditioned by this memory in a totally irrational way. Indeed the unconscious has its own logic.

The story of Martine, in Chapter 5 of *Free Your True Self 2* (abandonment experienced following the disappearance of the miller's son), is another example of a past life experience that can generate the development of an oral structure, specifically in terms of the sense of abandonment it activates. When the unconscious is emotionally charged with such experiences, one's daily living circumstances are perceived on the basis of this fear of deprivation, abandonment and loss. Furthermore, the energy contained in the active memory will tend to attract circumstances that will duplicate the same type of situations, not only during childhood, but throughout one's lifetime. If we recognise that there is no such thing as chance, we can see how our personal fate is shaped on the basis of very specific energy models.

4-3 Present life experiences which foster the recreation of an oral structure

In our observation, rarely were specific deprivations experienced at the time of conception or during the intra-uterine period. Generally speaking, nature ensures that the foetus has all it needs in physical terms, even at the expense of the mother. However, as soon as the child is born, there are plenty of occasions for experiencing deprivation and abandonment:

At birth, the child needs the presence of its mother physically, energetically and psychically; this is a genuine need without which it cannot thrive. Nature, in its infinite wisdom, has ensured that its needs are met by activating what we call the maternal instinct. Naturally and spontaneously, the mother will want to breastfeed her baby, to hold it close just after the birth and as often as possible during the course of the first year. Unfortunately, some rather different ideas were promoted in our materialistic society.

Thus, the conventional birth practices used in hospitals over the last fifty years have largely fostered the recreation of an oral structure.[1] First of all, at the physical level, when the umbilical cord is prematurely severed, this results in a brutal experience of separation, oxygen deprivation, and a sense of imminent death. Not only is that moment experienced as an assault (which reactivates a schizoid structure), but this brutal cutting off of life-giving nutrients can instantly reactivate past memories where the most essential survival needs were not met. The imprint of the fear related to physical survival is compounded by the fear of deprivation. This can also reactivate moments of brutal separation, cruel loss, and abandonment that were experienced in the past.

Then the newborn is generally washed, bundled up and separated from its mother, ending up alone in a crib. This conventional approach is based on the belief that once the child is born, it becomes an independent entity. The truth is, though an infant may survive physically, other aspects of its makeup suffer greatly from this separation. Indeed, though it may be out of its mother's womb, the infant is still linked to her etheric body. At this level, the link has not yet been severed, so that the infant needs to stay very close to her to continue to be fed energetically. Separation at this point confronts the infant with a painful experience of solitude, a sense of abandonment, and a cruel state of "affective" deprivation combined with energy deprivation. It is possible to reconnect with the memory of these specific moments in the birth process.[2] This experience of deprivation has been reported in thousands of cases.

Besides the physical circumstances, all the psychological conditions surrounding birth have a profound impact on the infant's psyche, as a result of its hypersensitivity. Bernard Montaud makes the following comments regarding an infant's fist contact with its parents:

Through those first hugs, an infant knows all there is to know about his father's and his mother's traumatic cycle. He can see them, and this knowledge sears through his being. Like most people, his parents are unaware of their imperfections, but to add to this, they are using his fresh new life to bolster their own lies. The infant doesn't get it: "What is this love? How do they love me? How do they love themselves?" But the horror doesn't stop there, for there is yet another dimension to it. Let us not forget that motherly love is all that he has left. That boundless cosmic warmth, that great nurturing love has vanished, to make way for motherly warmth. Motherly love is therefore his last resort. And this is precisely where the infant suffers the most crushing sense of abandonment and betrayal: the only loving solution he has left, his mother, ends up not being there.[3]

Though none of this is spectacular as seen from the outside, it is more than enough to create or reactivate past experiences of abandonment and devastating loss, which an infant carries within its memories.

The way that an infant is fed also plays a key role in the formation of this structure. Nature has given mothers the capacity to breastfeed their babies. From a purely materialistic perspective, mother's milk simply has a certain nutritional value, which is good for the infant's physical body. So if we find any other adequate substitute, this should not be a problem. Yet from the infant's perspective, this is indeed a serious problem, in energetic and psychic terms. First of all there is no great human warmth in a bottle; nor is there the quality of energy and love emanating from the mother, which a tiny, vulnerable infant so deeply needs. This is not just a matter of sentimentality: this is a genuine psychic need, and failure to meet this need will have very negative consequences. Even if the mother takes time to hold her baby in her arms, her milk has a quality of energy, which is quite different from "motherized" milk that is artificially reconstituted. In addition, at the tip of each breast, there is a small "chakra", an energy centre that feeds the infant's etheric body. When science eventually develops more refined analytical tools, it will recognize this as a matter of fact, rather than recommend bottle-feeding out of ignorance. Certainly if the mother, for some reason, is unable to breastfeed her baby, bottle-feeding will be a necessary and useful substitute. But apart from such cases, breastfeeding should be a matter of course, for the greater benefit of the child.

In fact, this long-standing recommended use of bottle-feeding in our society was not purely the result of ignorance. There were certain financial interests at stake. Indeed, a mother's milk costs nothing, and it contains antibodies that protect the infant from disease. It is available to all, makes people self-reliant, and nobody makes any money from it! On the other hand, buying the milk, the bottles, and all the other stuff required for bottle-feeding is totally in the interest of the large corporations that dominate today's market economy. Many people are becoming aware of this economic exploitation, which is founded on people's ignorance and can take many forms, to the detriment of our general health and well being. Meanwhile, an infant being fed milk from a bottle will generally feel this energetic deprivation, which can reactivate other memories of the same order.

During early childhood, especially from 0 to 2 years: with the birth trauma, this is the period when an oral structure will tend to be most deeply imprinted in an individual's consciousness. Indeed, at that moment, the child is totally dependent on others for physical and psychic nurturing. He has genuine needs in terms of his physical and psychological growth, and these are rarely fully met.

First, there are all these people who have had an "unhappy childhood". There is no need to go over all the pain and desperation that some children experience in the context of dysfunctional families, where they lack for everything, especially when it comes to nurturing contact and love. This structure does not need violence to begin to take shape. Violence during childhood will tend to lead to the development of the third and fifth structures (masochist and rigid), which will be examined further on. The parents' unavailability and negligence, whether real or apparent, will be enough to generate great suffering for the sense of deprivation is very real at that time.

It is worth noting that, although we may share the viewpoint according to which the soul chooses its childhood circumstances, this does not mean that we should do nothing to change these circumstances. On the contrary, through the situations laid out for us to experience, the soul creates opportunities to act, to learn, to change things, and to heal. This means that the more support these unloved children get, the quicker the healing of many past wounds will occur.

There are also all those who have grown up in apparently "normal" families, but where the parents' coldness, incompetence, physical or psychological unavailability, for all kinds of reasons, have led those children to feel a profound lack of affection or a sense of abandonment which have remained deeply embedded in their hearts. If a child carries within him a strong set of similar memories from past lives, even a brief stay with a neighbour or at a hospital at a very young age, as was the case with Charles, or a few months in a boarding school, or the temporary absence of a parent, may be interpreted by this child as a terrible experience of abandonment, even though the parents may have been reasonably affectionate.

4-4 The Oral Structure Defence System

> ✓ **The underlying fear of structure**: fear of deprivation, fear of loss, fear
> of abandonment
>
> ✓ **Emotional charge:** dissatisfaction, sense of emptiness, of deprivation, neediness, insecurity
>
> ✓ **Basic defence system:** stuffing, physical and emotional dependence
>
> ✓ **Statement of this structure:**
> "MORE!"<br>"I need more, feed me. Don't let me down; don't leave me."

4-5 Typical Behaviours of the Oral Structure

1) General attitude towards life:

The essential components of this dynamic, i.e. feelings of emptiness and loss, are such that any experience that can alleviate such feelings will bring pleasure, though the pleasure is very short-lived. This structure then generates general attitudes such as the following:

• Dissatisfaction

The permanent sense of emptiness is such that the individual will constantly seek fulfilment and well-being, through all kinds of activities, though he never seems to actually experience this. This is one of the main sources generating the cycle of dissatisfaction described earlier. One never has enough. Satisfaction is obviously impossible since the sense of deprivation springs from a basic wound that needs to be healed rather than from real deprivation of something external, which must be found. This unconscious dissatisfaction leads to a constant desire for stuffing with all kinds of things, in all aspects of daily living.

• Stuffing

This structure generates a behaviour called "stuffing", which we described in Chapter 2 of *Free Your True Self 2*, and which is so widespread in today's world. We saw that stuffing can be achieved through various means:

    —physical means: food, drink, tobacco, drugs, alcohol

—psychological means: television, shopping, hobbies, sports, politics, work, music, travels, studies, personal growth seminars, any activity, in fact, can be a source of stuffing for the oral structure

—energetic means: in the context of relationships with others, the individual "siphons" energy whenever possible

• Permanent insecurity

This insecurity does not stem from basic anxiety, as in the case of the schizoid structure, but from a fear of deprivation, of loss, of abandonment. So one is constantly seeking some form of pseudo-security in external circumstances (material circumstances or people). This generates all forms of dependency.

The feeling of insecurity also generates stress, which leads a person to want to **accumulate, hoard, and possess**, for the sake of self-preservation in case of future scarcity. A state of **permanent worry about the future** is thus created.

The inherent fears of this structure also generate **attachment and a fear of letting go**. The major illusion fostered by this structure is that one will eventually gain satisfaction when one finds the right person or the right thing (whatever that may be) in sufficient quantity.

• Dependency, parasitic behaviour

The sense of deprivation leads to a "parasitic" attitude, where the individual sucks other people's energy. A person who is caught in this structure is constantly "on the lookout for a provider", thus easily developing an attitude of dependency with regard to anyone or anything on whom or on which he might attach the illusion, or even worse, the hope of ever being satiated or content. This person thus lives in a constant state of expectation, which also generates inner stress and tension.

• Blame and victimitis

Since one does not understand why one is always so unsatisfied, one generally blames others or situations for not providing the satisfaction one so desperately needs. This is one of the two structures that generate a victim's behaviour, such as described in another of my books (*The Power of Free Will*, chapter 4).

• Excess

This incessant pursuit of unattainable satisfaction obviously generates a dynamic for all kinds of excesses: excess in food, sex, work, shopping, television watching, excess in all areas where the individual has chosen to compensate for his sense of emptiness.
No matter what he does, an individual caught in an oral structure will always push the envelope. If it's stuffing through work, he will work ceaselessly like a maniac. Though people may urge him to slow down—and this is something he

will definitely want to do once he becomes aware of the problem—he just "cannot stop himself" from working, as if driven by something "stronger and bigger than himself". He is caught in a similar mechanism to the one that drives a person to eat too much, to smoke or to do anything that one might unsuccessfully want to stop.[5]

The same goes for any chosen method of stuffing. Some are more acceptable than others in our society, but they are nevertheless damaging, in the long or short term. Stuffing can take the form of shopping or television watching. These are well perceived activities that are in fact encouraged in our consumer society, though they generate a great deal of misery and alienation. The most destructive aspect, in this case, is that the people engaging in this form of stuffing generally do not even realise that they are caught in a mechanism. They don't draw any link between this inner mechanism and the trouble they have in achieving a happy and fulfilling life. Problems such as bulimia or alcoholism are fairly obvious. But it is very rare to hear about a problem of dependency related to shopping or television, for example. Yet this dynamic is very harmful and destructive.

This dissatisfaction and permanent sense of deprivation are such that the person is constantly out to take rather than give, since giving is experienced as a loss, a major ordeal. One might say that such a person is selfish, but this judgement is clearly uncalled for. There is no ill will here, just a person caught in a mechanism stemming from his/her past, one that the person is usually totally unaware of.

We all have this structure more or less active within us, and it is interesting to note our behaviours, our motivation, and our reactions to the world around us in order to catch a glimpse of their presence. As for any other structure, the "witness stance", a constant state of vigilance and sincerity with oneself will quickly lead to a realisation of just how active this structure is within us. For some, this is a minor structure with no determining influence. For others, it is a dominant structure, and liberation from this dynamic is a major step towards experiencing happiness and freedom.

Let us now observe how these general behavioural aspects are translated in certain areas of daily living.

2) Relationships
A DEPRIVED, HUNGRY, WORRIED, DEPENDENT HEART

More...

Fear of losing, possessiveness, insecurity, or attachment. In a couple relationship, a person who is caught in this defence system will tend to behave as follows:

—**demands satisfaction from the other** (i.e. that the other fills the emptiness and provides physical and emotional security); unconsciously perceives the other as a provider at every level, as a source of emotional and energetic stuffing, or any other source of satisfaction and security;

—**always wants more**; lives in a constant state of expectation, either verbally or energetically expressed: more attention, more love, more approval, more sex, more;

—**is permanently frustrated**, since the individual feels as if he is never getting enough;

—**blames** his partner for his dissatisfaction;

—clings and hangs on, since his greatest fear is that of abandonment; lives in a state of dependency; will therefore have a lot of trouble ending a relationship, even if it is evidently not working out and hopeless; keeps on hoping and will never let go; anything is better than the feeling of losing or parting;

—tries to control his partner so as to be sure of not losing his source of survival; insecurity and fear of losing lead to possessiveness and jealousy;

—manipulates in sweet, tortuous and hidden ways so as to get the satisfaction he wants;

—is very burdensome in a couple relationship;

—is often tired and lacking energy;

—gives little or, if there is giving, it is with the hope of substantial returns; takes in all kinds of ways;

—seeks emotional or energetic "merging", which is only one more way to take the other person's energy, a way of binding the other person in order to be sure not to lose him/her;

—is prone to selfishness;

—seeks commitment and fidelity as a way to bind the other person rather than as a free and healthy commitment;

—faces conflicts through sweet manipulation and indolence; complains and asks for more; doesn't fight directly, unless other structures generate anger;

—is very nice, caring and pleasant, as long as there is hope for some form of future satisfaction; but after several unmet expectations, can become an unpleasant, guilt-wielding pain in the neck; "siphons" even more energy with unstated criticisms, furtive disapproving looks and sighs;

—does not like groups, but hates solitude just as much; prefers being in the company of just one person. This allows him to better experience the contact, but also to pump the other's energy more easily.

3) Sexuality

Sexual activity, which brings a momentary but powerful feeling of satisfaction and fulfilment on a physical level, will be easily reclaimed so as to fill this sense of emptiness. In addition, during sex, there is an energy exchange that can lead to stuffing with the other person's energy. So there is a great deal of interest in sex. In particular, if the memory leans more towards stuffing than a sense of abandonment, there will be people for whom sex is of primary importance. The energy of the second chakra, which is highly charged, will be used for intense sexual activity. If the individual does not have a permanent partner, he will be perpetually on the make trying to find someone, looking at any person of the opposite sex (or the same sex, depending on preferences) as a potential sexual partner.

Sexual relationships easily create energetic links. If the active memory within this structure leans more towards the sense of abandonment, it will be easy to create an even stronger state of emotional dependency coupled with energetic bonds. Sex then becomes a trap fostering possessiveness and jealousy, making people dependent and strongly (and painfully) attached to their partner.

Yet as with any other mechanism, the individual will never be really satisfied and will go on always wanting more, no matter what the quality of the previous interaction may have been. Frustration (which is only an expression of a basic sense of deprivation) will very quickly reappear. An extraordinary sexual encounter will create even higher expectations for the next time (which should not be too far away). For this reason, the individual experiences his own sexuality in a perpetual state of insecurity, deprivation, fear and stress. A fully satisfying, unfettered and happy sexual relationship becomes impossible, no matter what the circumstances or who the partner(s) may be.

4) Physical body
• Body shape

This structure often results in rounded body shapes, which does not necessarily mean overweight, depending on the type of stuffing used.

• Health

First of all, the structure will lead to illnesses which correspond to the types of excess it generates. If the stuffing used is of a physical nature, we may find all the problems related to physical excess in its various forms (excess food or inappropriate food, alcohol, tobacco, prescription drugs, recreational drugs, etc.). Food is a preferred way to experience the pleasure of stuffing in response to a sense of need (an empty stomach instantly activates the memory of need and deprivation within the unconscious), and to trigger dependency. For example, the person "cannot help eating"; even foods he knows very well are bad for his health, as he struggles with this unconscious mechanism.

Often, along with excess intake of food comes excess weight. It is easy to see how difficult it is for these people to stick to a diet. As long as the memories remain active, doing without certain foods through a conscious act of will is tantamount to acting against the will of the unconscious structure, which, as we know, is generally much stronger than conscious will. This is a losing battle, a source of repeated disappointments and discouraging failures. Many people who have a weight problem fight hard and spend fortunes, including, in some cases, the expense of painful surgical operations, in order to "stop feeling hungry", most often with temporary or limited results. In my practice, I have observed that it is infinitely more effective to deal with the source of the desire for food which, in fact, has little to do with one's stomach. The weight problem naturally disappears the moment one defuses the memory in which the problem is rooted. The same goes for other types of stuffing.

As the sense of dissatisfaction and the fear of loss generated by this structure create a permanent state of tension, we might also encounter various diseases related to stress and frustration.

• Automatic choices in clothing

Generally speaking, an oral person will not be overly concerned with external appearance, beauty or image-consciousness. He will therefore not pay much attention to clothes. His preferred way of getting attention, of taking other people's energy, is more focused on a psychological attitude than on manipulation through external appearance. On the other hand, he may be compulsively on the lookout for comfort, spending fortunes on comfortable clothes, or instead spend very little on cheap clothes, in order to save money. The structure constantly swings between insecurity and the sense of deprivation. An oral person will therefore often have a rather full wardrobe. He buys clothes on sale even when he doesn't need them, just so as not to miss the opportunity. He is a bargain hunter. He keeps clothes for years, even when he no longer wears them, and has a lot of trouble clearing out his closets. As for many other material things, he does not want to risk doing without something in case of some future need.

5) The energy aspect

The oral structure tends to concentrate energy at the level of the belly. In the presence of an oral structure, one senses a heavy, lukewarm, sticky, draining kind of energy. In any interaction, the individual will tend to stare at the other person in order to siphon as much energy as possible through the eyes. He will often speak in low tones so that one is forced to really listen and be attentive to what he is saying in order to grab one's attention and extract more energy.

Like the schizo, but for different reasons, an oral person is quickly tired. He is indolent, slow to act, dragging his feet and hoping that some day life will be great and he will finally be able to celebrate it with a total sense of security and fulfilment.

6) Relating to the material world and money

An oral structure generates an "ideal", compulsive consumer, as we saw in Chapter 2 of *Free Your True Self 2*. Its inherent permanent state of emptiness leads to constant buying to fill one's body, one's house, one's time, one's heart, to fill the silence and solitude of one's life. Anything that gives an impression of emptiness must be filled.

The fear of loss and insecurity regarding the future will tend to lead to avarice. Often, an oral person will put money aside for "the golden years", or will spend a lifetime in stress for the sake of tomorrow. Yet at the same time, he is unaware of the way he relates to money. (Let us not forget that a mechanism lodged in the unconscious distorts reality, and therefore blocks any chance of remaining objective.) He will feel torn between the desire to accumulate money (insecurity) and the desire to consume for the sake of stuffing (sense of emptiness). He will save on small things, then spend a fortune on other things that have no greater useful purpose. This generates totally contradictory behaviours which have little to do with conscious and intelligent choices, but a great deal to do with the way the mechanism works whenever a situation arises.

7) Relating to power
• Using other people's power

External manifestations of the power to act and make decisions are of little interest to this structure unless they can generate a sense of security (which will, of course, remain an illusion). Instead of seeking power directly, an oral person will tend to manipulate or to latch onto someone who seems to have power (i.e. energy, in some form or other), in order to get as much as possible in return. Taking on power is far too demanding, and in any case he just doesn't have it in him, since he doesn't have enough energy by himself.

• Domination for the sake of not losing

In the context of intimate relationships, an oral person will try to dominate his partner or his children in order to preserve the stock of energy represented in the person, to maintain a good supply. This has more to do with attachment and possession than with direct domination.

• Loss of power and autonomy through dependency

The oral structure carries within it a declaration of powerlessness to generate satisfaction on its own. It leads to a refusal to take responsibility for one's own well being, and thus to **the loss of one's own power and autonomy**. The unconscious looks for a provider in some form or other. Dependency is generated not only in the context of intimate relationships but in all kinds of situations:

    —dependency regarding work (the fear of loss is very active, especially these days when everything seems so unstable);

    —physical dependency, as we saw earlier with regard to health issues;

    —emotional dependency, which doesn't just focus on the partner. It turns up at all levels, especially in relation to any authority figure who, as far as the unconscious is concerned, represents the parent who did not give what should have been given during childhood. This explains, in particular, the "guru" phenomenon, whether the guru is authentic or not, with his army of "devotees" who stand ready to do anything just to get a little energy from the "divine" teacher. There will be jostling and trampling and fighting just for the privilege of filling oneself with a look, a touch, a blessing, while being totally unaware of the obvious transgression of the very teachings extolled by the master (if indeed he or she is a genuine master), i.e. respect for one another, dignity, sharing, inner silence, and emotional stillness. Yet the moment the structure is activated, one quickly forgets all those beautiful teachings, as one becomes the puppet of the oral mechanism: "I am in need, so please fill me."

If the person to whom one turns for this kind of stuffing, and to whom one confers all one's personal power, is not a guru, several other forms of authority will do, such as doctors, members of the government, the mother, the boss, or any form of provider/authority on whom to tack one's expectations.

Then, after many dashed hopes and expectations, one might decide to change the source (find another spouse, guru, therapist), and the expectation/frustration mechanism will kick in once again.

• Loss of power from being easily manipulated

While the oral structure often takes the form of manipulation, it can also lead a person to be easily manipulated (as is true of all the other mechanisms). The world has plenty of manipulators, as we shall see with other structures (especially the psychopathic and the rigid structures) who love to feed off such easy prey. The latter are obviously no more to blame, since we are all miserable as long as we remain caught in these structures, whether we are among the manipulators or the manipulated. These are just different ways of being miserable.

Because of this permanent state of deprivation and expectation, it is very easy to manipulate an oral person by fostering the hope that some day his every need will be fulfilled. False gurus promise enlightenment and boundless blessings; our society promises happiness through consumption. The mechanism works individually as well as collectively.

8) Work

Only rarely will a person who is caught in an oral structure be seen creating his own individual projects. He has no energy to give, so he has to find a situation where he can be the taker. Generally speaking, he will prefer the role of an employee or sidekick, so as to take as much and give as little as possible without risk. He will try to benefit as much as possible in any situation: financial benefits, a nicer office, more holidays, a better parking space, time off, all kinds of benefits, large and small. All that matters is that he gets the feeling of receiving. Of course, there again, he will feel that his boss or his provider doesn't give enough, and will find ways to need more and to remain in a constant state of frustration.

9) Service

Service, as an opportunity to give generously without expectations, will not interest an oral personality in the least.

10) Pitfalls in spiritual seeking

The dynamic involving stuffing and dependency is also found here. As we mentioned earlier, the quest for a spiritual teacher can easily be reclaimed by this structure. This can be a totally appropriate quest as long as it safeguards the devotee's autonomy and independence and leads him to the point of becoming his own master. We all need instructors and people more advanced than ourselves who can inspire us through their teachings and their example. But an oral personality can easily reclaim this quest by projecting all of his unresolved emotional needs onto the "guru", thereby feeding the structure instead of unravelling it. How easy it is for the unconscious to project the image of the father or mother on these "teachers" who seem so full of love and compassion, and who seem to be speaking just for us. This is one of the major pitfalls of the oral structure.

In the context of personal development courses, the individual will look for places where there is a lot of sentimental outpouring, with lots of hugs and physical contacts. He will also love wealth building and prosperity-oriented courses.[6] Apart from these, his favourite workshops and seminars may be courses in massage and other very physical approaches. Obviously, if a person uses such teachings to feed his structure, the benefits he will derive will be minimal. The issue is not the nature of the teachings or courses, but the motivation and awareness with which they are approached.

11) Some practical suggestions and tasks leading to transformation

In order to liberate oneself from an oral structure, one must look inward to find one's own source of energy and well being, stop being emotionally and energetically dependent on things or people, liberate oneself from attachment out of fear of loss, learn to let go and to give without expectations, trust in life, create one's own inner security, **recover a sense of fulfilment regardless of outer circumstances**, become a free being and let others be free.

In day to day living, one might start undoing an oral structure by developing rigor and awareness in one's spending habits: learn to distinguish between real needs and automatic demands springing from the ego, question oneself regarding the pertinence of certain forms of stuffing that could be stopped relatively easily. Other needs, which are more deeply rooted in one's unconscious, will have to be unravelled at their source, through specific inner work. For this reason, one should avoid excessive rigor. One needs to give oneself a lot of love, and even permissions, as this can be very useful in this process.

One can also begin to liberate oneself from emotional dependency by getting involved in soul-nourishing activities (art is a very healing activity); by taking part in external service activities (volunteering can be very beneficial, as it involves giving of oneself), and creative activities where one can experience the joy of giving generously while developing one's creativity; by finding inspiration in examples of devotion, detachment, and generous action. This allows one to sense one's own inner wealth, while it fosters the emergence of a very nurturing and higher form of energy.

4-6 The Oral Structure Transformed

What could be lacking
for the man who has placed himself beyond all desires?
What external resource might he need
if he has gathered within himself all of his wealth?
—Seneca

• Qualities

The qualities found here are often the opposite of the structure in its hardened form. This is particularly evident in the case of an oral person. When the structure is tempered, the individual **becomes open, relaxed, and celebrates each living moment** as it is, without expectations. In this way, he becomes free again to fully enjoy every minute of his daily life.

This relaxed attitude, this trust in life makes the person **generous, kind, caring, nurturing**, aware of other people and their needs, and able to help without keeping tabs. He also becomes aware of his real needs and is easily content. He is very pleasant company, with an easy way of undramatising situations, **laughing, playful, light-hearted and inspiring** in his high spirits. He becomes a perfect example of best features of the jovial "bon vivant".

Being an **autonomous** and complete being, he no longer creates alienating attachments for himself or for others. This is yet another area where he finds renewed freedom while also letting others be free. He now feels loved and is able to love unconditionally.

The sense of deprivation is transformed into a profound sense of the abundance and generosity of the Universe. The individual is now able to generate a satisfying life in concrete ways at all levels. This is genuine affluence, not through an accumulation of material possessions, which is a false form of affluence, but through the ability to enjoy life as it is, without wanting more. And in such cases, life often brings us more.

• Declaration of transformation

When the structure is defused, one can finally experience genuine fulfilment, no matter what the circumstances may be. Through this renewed contact with the wealth of the soul, one can now declare:

> "No matter what the circumstances may be, I am content; I am self-reliant and free; I live in affluence; I let others be free; I don't need others; I find my own source of contentment within me, and I share it abundantly with others; I am inwardly full and rich, and I share this wealth by making generous contributions to the world; I can do this because life is filled with abundance and I am in contact with my inner, infinite source."

• Contribution task

When transformed, this structure is a blessing in our society. These are the people who contribute the most, through their example, to the development of a community characterised by freedom, awareness and abundance, where there would be no need to wallow in material things in order to derive some semblance of contentment, a society where each person would create his or her own fulfilment through contact with the soul, where each of us could manifest our essential generosity, our goodness, our joy of living in total trust regarding the future. As an antidote to our consumer society, a transformed oral person brings a sense of contentment with limited external means, laying the groundwork for building a new world. This state of mind leads to the creation of abundance for all.

4-7 The Oral Structure – Summary

- **Basic fear of the structure:** fear of deprivation, of abandonment
- **Source experiences in the past:** deprivation, loss, abandonment
- **Emotional charge:** fear of losing, sense of emptiness, insecurity
- **Defence system:** stuffing, dependency, selfishness, attachment, parasitic behaviour, excess
- **Declaration of the defence system:** "More... I need more... I don't have enough... don't leave me..."
- **Needed work:** get rid of the fear of deprivation and the fear of loss; learn to be content in any circumstance.
- **Declaration of transformation:**

> I am totally content.

- **Fundamental quality of the soul to be recovered:**

> FULFILMENT

- **Qualities of the structure, once transformed:**

GENEROSITY, kindness, gentleness, relaxed state of being; nurturing attitude, will be able to take care of others while letting them be free, a healing, cheerful and balanced person.

- **Contribution task:**

> Bring a sense of abundance into the world

Bravo, that's enough for you orals!

— · — · — · — · — · — · — · — · — · —

[1] Fortunately, as we mentioned in our presentation of the schizoid structure, things are changing. But the fact remains that we are part of the one or two generations of the western world who went through this type of birth experience.

[2] In particular, working with one's breath, as we will see later in this book, can often bring such experiences within conscious awareness.

[3] Bernard Montaud, op.cit. Chapter 4.

[4] Annie Marquier, *The Power of Free Will*, Chapter 4.

[5] As is the case with other structures, one does not change through an act of conscious will, since the unconscious emotional charge is generally too strong and one drives oneself to exhaustion, with very little results. Genuine change will require that we defuse the active memory lodged in the unconscious through specific inner work.

[6] Within the New Age movement, there is a vast selection of books and courses to learn to generate prosperity, to realize one's dreams. This is a valid effort to counteract certain false ideas circulating on this subject among ordinary people, and develop an awareness of other perspectives. On the other hand, many people will get lost in this quest and become mired in illusion even more if they don't take the trouble to **sincerely examine their motivation** for seeking prosperity and realizing their dreams. Does this desire truly spring from the soul, to be in a better position to make a positive contribution in the world, or does the desire spring from a personality that is caught up in fears and insecurity

chapter 5

The MASOCHIST Structure
FEELING CRUSHED, POWERLESS, VICTIMIZED
"Poor me"

5-1 Stories

Mary had a stressful childhood. Her father was authoritarian, and she was always terrified of him. Her mother was often sick, and she had a sad, tired outlook on life, always on the lookout for some new calamity. In fact, Mary never saw her mother happy. She learned at a very young age that life is no fun. Joy and pleasure were totally absent from her home. As her mother was always sick or exhausted, she was the one who had to care for her five brothers and sisters most of the time, since she was the eldest child. Quivering before fatherly authority, she always submitted, out of fear. As a teenager, she found that dating was out of the question, since there were far too many things to do at home. Her friends would invite her but she always refused, knowing that, in any case, her father would object and her mother would whine if she went. A sad and crushing childhood, and a busy adolescence had been her lot in life.

Now an adult, Mary has a good job. She works as an agent in an institution providing care to the handicapped. She is discreet and very efficient. Her boss is very happy with her, as she does all that is asked of her without balking, and does it well. She is a model employee. Yet she always feels sad and often tired. She doesn't like to go out, and has very few friends. At the moment, she is single and she is likely to stay that way for a long while since she takes little pleasure in the company of men. She is small and rather skinny, doesn't really take care of her appearance, which remains simple to the point of austerity, and which ultimately doesn't make her very attractive. With each passing year, she is becoming more and more impatient and bitter. Nothing ever works out the way she would like, and she finds life profoundly unfair. She spends her time complaining for one reason or another. Her younger colleagues get on her nerves. In fact, a seething jealousy is eating her up inside, especially for the girl who has such a great husband and two beautiful children and who always comes to work in a cheerful mood. She never misses a chance to fire unpleasant remarks at her, or to subtly sabotage her work on occasion. Over time, her whole being has become hardened in a negative attitude. In addition, her health has not been the best lately. She is getting thinner day-by-day, and has stomach ulcers. But she blames other people whenever she feels in pain. She is such a generous and helpful person, how could life be so unfair and so difficult for her? It's because people are mean, selfish, ungrateful, and life is a bitch.

Mary could thus spend her life in utter frustration and sadness, wordlessly keeping her suffering bottled up inside of her, unless something happens to initiate a basic transformation of her inner structure.

◆   ◆   ◆

Peter is an only child, who was raised by a very authoritarian mother and an indolent father, who came alive only when he came home drunk. He would then have violent arguments with his wife and use this as an excuse to beat his son. Peter learned to crawl before his father's violent temper and his mother's authority. She, in particular, imposed a strict code of behaviour in every detail. Never would he be allowed to dress as he wanted, and he had to go to school dressed according to her taste, which often made him feel ridiculous in the eyes of his peers. He had tried to object, but she had been inflexible. In addition, she would force him to eat foods he didn't like, and she would often forbid him to go and play with his friends whom she considered inappropriate. At such times, he hated her to the point of wishing she would vanish from his life. He nevertheless had to submit to her authority throughout his childhood.

As soon as he became a teenager, however, he became very rebellious. He left home and learned to fend for himself. After a few job experiences, he was smart enough, and aggressive enough, to carve himself a niche in the business world. He managed to set up an import-export company that is now fairly successful. He works long hours, yet he can't seem to keep his associates. He is very demanding and quick to anger when things don't turn out the way he wants them to. He constantly complains about the state of the economy, about incompetent employees, unfavourable circumstances that keep turning up and undermining his efforts to truly succeed. If only we had different people in the government, more honest mechanics, less arrogant women, more responsible young people, less lousy weather, a less idiotic dog, then maybe life might be somewhat acceptable. But present conditions are just impossible and he can't do anything about them, other than use every chance he gets to complain and bitch against everything and anything.

Despite his dour disposition, he manages to get married. But after the usual first idyllic months, he begins to voice various complaints to his wife. No matter what she does, he always finds something to pick at. He subjects her to a constant flow of criticism, either directly or indirectly, through his bad moods. When she protests, he throws outrageous fits, which he often regrets afterwards. He is very tough on his children, always unsatisfied with their behaviour, trying to bend them to his expectations, constantly angered by their carelessness. Over time, he becomes more and more bitter and more and more prone to violent outbursts. Alcohol is no longer enough to put him in a good mood. On the contrary, it seems to fuel the constant anger he carries within him. He doesn't understand what is going on. He feels unhappy, frustrated, and yet on those rare occasions when he manages to see his predicament from a more objective standpoint, he can see that he doesn't really have any reason to feel so miserable and angry with the world. He begins to feel a terrible tension in his shoulders, as well as chronic back pains that are more and more painful to him, and are making him more and more impatient. Things are going from bad to worse. When will it ever end?

Peter and Mary are caught in the "masochist" structure. Their behaviour illustrates just a few of its aspects. Its fundamental characteristic is a profound **sense**

of powerlessness and despondency, in the face of uncontrollable circumstances, that generate **fear and seething anger, which may or may not be externalised**.

This structure can also be defined as that of the "victim", in the broader sense of the term. It is so widespread and destructive that I have focused an entire book on this topic, entitled *The Power of Free Will*, where I offer a new dynamic of consciousness in order to effectively defuse this structure. We are all more or less affected by "victimitis", and getting rid of this dynamic represents a major step towards inner liberation.

5-2 Past life experiences at the root of the masochist structure

Our observation has shown that this mechanism is rooted in two types of experiences: that of the victim and that of the perpetrator.

The first type of past experience: the VICTIM

Such are the experiences of a person who was crushed by some power, who had to submit unwillingly to that power, and was mistreated and exploited without any means of self-protection or self-defence. The traumatic source of this structure therefore stems from situations where one has been subjected to **abuse of power, disrespect for one's dignity, suppression of freedom, and personal annihilation, in a state of near total physical or psychological powerlessness.**

Martha is a submissive, shy young girl. In early childhood, she had had a lot of trouble learning to speak. Her parents could not understand this "impairment". In fact, she only began to speak somewhat adequately around the age of five. A discreet person, she lived in fear of others and never dared to stand up to anybody, especially her father, a very authoritarian fellow. The children were not allowed to speak at the dinner table, and had to submit to paternal authority without discussion. She never dared to ask for anything. There was one time, however, at the age of fourteen, when she took the chance of asking for permission to go to a friend's birthday party. Her father's categorical refusal frightened her so much that she waited until she was twenty four years old before she dared once again to ask permission to go out. Throughout her adult life, she was very limited in her ability to express herself verbally, as if words were somehow prevented from leaving her mouth. She would have liked to learn foreign languages, but found it so extremely difficult that she gave up on the idea. She could not understand why life was so difficult for her, and she felt very frustrated by this situation. Martha was caught in a masochist structure, with all the behaviours it entails. She never dared to stand up for herself, yet was constantly judging others, and a seething anger was beginning to boil within her. She would repress this, of course, since she was far too afraid of self-expression, and no one could tell how she felt. But she was going downhill more and more. She then decided to do some inner work in order to stop being afraid, to regain a measure of self-confidence and joy of living. In due course, the following memories emerged:

The setting was in France, around the fifteenth century. She was a servant in a convent. She knew she had been abandoned by her mother and that the nuns had taken her in. As a "child born of sin", she was subjected to every form of vexation throughout her childhood, having to work at household chores and in the kitchen from the age of five. Everyone treated her with utter contempt. In particular, she was not allowed to speak to her superiors, or to even look them in the eyes. She was expected to bow her head whenever her path crossed theirs, which was to be avoided as much as possible. One day, she dared to mention to a visiting high ranking member of the clergy that one of her work mates was ill and needed care. The prelate fired a look of devastating contempt at her. Later on, she was summoned by the mother superior, who gave a brutal warning to the effect that if she ever dared to do that again, she would be kicked out, and that, for this time, she would be punished. She was beaten and sentenced to a month in confinement, in a cold damp cell, with almost nothing to eat. She caved in, and never said another word. Thus she lived in fear of authority, scorned in her dignity, and finally died in her twenties for lack of care.

◆ ◆ ◆

Sonia is also caught in a masochist structure. She is married to a man who is rigid and cold. For years, she tried to have children, and had four consecutive miscarriages before finally giving birth to a daughter. Throughout her pregnancy, Sonia hardly had the strength to stand, and had to lie down most of the time. Childbirth didn't help things either, and she is totally exhausted. She has repeated liver attacks, and her health is extremely delicate. Any little setback drags her down, and the least effort is exhausting to her. She tries all kinds of ways to take care of herself, but nothing seems to work. She looks like she is always on the verge of fainting. Her general behaviours are those of a passive victim: "Poor me, why me, life is hard and unfair; I'm doing all I can but I am a victim of outrageous fortune." Eventually, she recalled the following memory:

As a young girl, she lived in a small village in the Middle Ages. She became pregnant out of wedlock. When the villagers became aware of her condition, they showered her with insults and contempt. One day, three men came to her home and forced her to go with them to a shack in the woods. Once there, they verbally and physically abused her and raped her, as punishment for her sin. They then locked her up in the shack. They came back to abuse her several times until, fearing discovery, they killed her and got rid of her body.

Sonia came back carrying not only a terrible unconscious fear of pregnancy, but also a fear of any power stronger than her, a profound sense of powerlessness, and seething anger. In fact, from the moment her child was born, she unconsciously, constantly feared the same horrible reprisal she had experienced in the past. The mere presence of the child would reactivate this fear, combined with a sense of indignity, powerlessness and anger that would drain her of all her energy and make her sick (those liver attacks). There was nothing rational about this. There was no justification for this in her present life. But, as we have seen, the lower mind, which harbours our unconscious memories, is anything but rational. It has its own logic.

If we look at the history of mankind until today, we can easily come across stories of abuse of power. History, in fact, seems mostly filled with these kinds of events:

— collectively: savage enemy invasions, involving looting and massacres, tyrannical governments, slavery, prostitution, poor people abused by the rich, all manner of exploitation of the weak by the strong;

— individually: one can easily imagine all kinds of violent abuse of power, for example a slave who is beaten, exploited, forced to work beyond the limits of his strength, sexually abused, having his human dignity put down on a daily basis for years and years; or a woman who lives under the boot of a violent husband, abused, scorned, gagged, psychologically imprisoned; or a family invaded by an enemy who forces them into treason under threat of torture, who treats the vanquished in shameful ways, etc. Sexual abuses, in particular, are painfully experienced as violations of personal freedom and dignity, that directly affect the most vulnerable aspects of one's being, both physically and psychologically. They are always accompanied by a painful sense of powerlessness. There are also less obvious forms of abuse of power, that wear a person down day by day, week by week, and are no less destructive: parents abusing children, a boss abusing his employees, masters abusing servants, the strong abusing the weak, the powers that be abusing the man in the street, all forms of abuse perpetrated by those who hold power over those who don't. The whole spectrum of suffering and injustice generated by the abuse of power is the stuff of countless novels. In the context of these stories, whenever an arch-villain is described, it is always someone who has power and who abuses that power. By the way, the reason those novels are so compelling to read is that they actually tell our own story.

Inner consequences of past experiences of this type:

Each time we suffered as a result of being **crushed in our dignity and stifled in our freedom**, an emotional construct developed in the unconscious involving **a sense of desperation with regard to one's own powerlessness and a violent rebellion against this abuse of power**. The lower mind is then loaded with a double mechanism that will become a defence system:

1. **submission**, fear, sense of powerlessness, despair, sadness, loss of confidence in one's own power, repressed anger;

2. **rebellion**, anger, rage and aggressiveness.

The second type of past experience: the PERPETRATOR

This type of experience may seem the opposite of the victim's structure. Yet it is very often its source, springing from a mechanism of consciousness that leads an individual to swing between the opposite poles of "dominator vs. dominated". The experience of one or several lifetimes as a perpetrator may lead to choosing the life of a powerless, downtrodden and suffering victim. Indeed abusing power with impunity generates the following dynamics: on the one hand, there comes a point when one begins to feel a sense of guilt; on the other hand, **the law of learning (rather than punishment)** that is karma will kick in, as one has transgressed the laws of respect and love. There is a lesson to be learned. For this reason, after several lifetimes as a "perpetrator", the soul will generate situations which will allow the individual to change that tendency. It is then possible that the soul will arrange for the personality to have a direct experience of what it feels like to be subjected to abusive power.[1]

If the ego is sufficiently evolved, it can then learn the lesson, through this lifetime of disempowerment, by realising the importance of respect. This lesson will remain deeply imprinted within it, as it is now the outcome of experience. This is how inner strength and truth are built at every level. In this case, the test of power will certainly come up again in a subsequent lifetime, but the individual will then be able to approach it with a greater measure of wisdom and love.

If the ego is not yet sufficiently evolved, then this new lifetime as a victim will be an occasion to build, once again, a violent hatred towards any form of power, along with a strong desire to gain power for oneself, to get revenge and to never again be subjected to such debasement. The soul then allows the ego to build another lifetime as a perpetrator. Thus the wheel turns, through the centuries, in a **perpetrator-victim cycle**, each time affording **the chance to experience and to develop a little more awareness**, until one is finally able to extricate oneself from the cycle.[2] The following story is a good example of this:

Tom is caught in an active masochist structure. Without actually trying, he has managed to spontaneously recall a chain of past lives which effectively illustrate this cycle: while he was the son of a king, back in antiquity, his father was dethroned by invaders who took over the kingdom. Being tall and strong, he was sent as a rower on a galley for the rest of his life. The rage and hatred built up over this lifetime led to the creation of a subsequent lifetime as a violent and abusive pirate, captain of a faithless and lawless crew that roamed the seas. To compensate for this violence, several lifetimes later, he found himself a poor and sickly fisherman in Brittany, having to work for an authoritarian, ungrateful ship owner. This gave him another opportunity to stir up his anger towards power.

In his present lifetime, Tom is a representative for a distribution company dealing in frozen seafood. He doesn't particularly like his job, but everyone has to earn a living, right? He tried several times to change jobs, but it never worked out. It was as if something forced him to stay put. So he spends his time bitching about late deliveries, an unfair boss, and life in general, which is no picnic. He is unpleasant with everybody except people in authority, before whom he tends to squirm while gritting his teeth. He is atrocious with his wife and children, being constantly annoyed and frustrated. The least little thing can trigger violent outbursts of anger. His job involves meeting many people, so he often finds himself in the company of several people over lunch in a restaurant.

After a few drinks, he tends to spill out all his dissatisfaction with the rotten world in which we live, stating that a revolution is just about the only way to set things straight. He finds life hard, his clients too demanding, his colleagues incompetent and selfish, and he is getting fed up with talking about lobsters and shrimp day in and day out.

When he decided to work on this deep-seated dissatisfaction with life, he realised that his problem had nothing to do with lobsters, shrimp, and clients. By healing his past, he was able to change jobs very easily. Indeed, as soon as the inner work of defusing the structure was done, a fortunate "twist of fate" led to a meeting with a friend who offered him a position abroad in his company, which was something he had always dreamed about. And most importantly, he was able to recover an inner sense of joy and freedom that he had never known up to that point.

Thus, when it so happens that we conjure up memories as "poor victims", we can be sure that we also have some memories as "merciless perpetrators", hidden somewhere in our unconscious, that are far more difficult to acknowledge: our culture easily accepts the victim's position and actually takes pity on it, while casting a very negative judgement on perpetrators. Victims and perpetrators are two sides of the same coin, when examined from the perspective of evolution through the wheel of incarnations. This is how learning takes place. This teaches us to stop identifying with past lives. We are not those personalities, any more than we are this present personality. Our soul is simply gathering experiences through each of these personalities. On the other hand, **we are still responsible for each of these personalities**. If the brakes on our car no longer work properly, it is our responsibility to have them repaired before we become a public menace.

Whether the masochist structure is built as a result of past experiences as victims, or through reactions to activities associated with perpetrators, the behaviours resulting from this structure are the same, for they are based on the same attitude of the powerless, submissive, and rebellious victim, filled with either repressed or outwardly expressed rage and anger.

As we can see from Martha's story, and the same holds true for other structures, the soul will generate childhood circumstances that will tend to create a resonance between the lower mind and this type of active memory which lay embedded in the personal or collective unconscious.[3] Or circumstances that might be considered near "normal" will be interpreted as abuse of power if the unconscious is particularly charged with this kind of memory.

5-3 Present life experiences which foster the recreation of a masochist structure

Among the factors that reactivate this type of memory, we have observed few conditions having to do with intra-uterine life. On the other hand, it is very easy to reactivate them from the moment of birth, and then on through early childhood, since at those times, the personality is physically in a state of real vulnerability, and mistreatment can easily occur.

• Birth

Hospital birth conditions which have been common practice over the last fifty years, and which we have already described in the context of the first two structures, will also tend to reactivate memories related to the masochist structure. Indeed, from the beginning of the first contractions right through the entire birth process, the infant finds himself in a situation involving total powerlessness at the psychic level.

When he comes out of the mother's womb, he finds himself at the mercy of adults who have complete power over his fate. We know that a newborn child is hyperconscious and hypersensitive in his tiny body. If forceps must be used, for example, the infant experiences a very painful physical assault, and there is nothing he can do about it. He doesn't know that this may be for his own good. All that registers is that **it hurts and he cannot defend himself**. That is the moment when more ancient memories can be reactivated. If, in this case, the individual has an active memory relating to a time when he was stoned to death, and his head was crushed by a large rock, this similar sensation will automatically reactivate the fear, the powerlessness, the inner protest and the panic experienced at that moment. And even if the birth process occurs without any outside intervention, the process itself is uncomfortable for the child, and this can spontaneously reactivate memories.

The premature cutting of the umbilical cord before it stops beating is another activating factor for this structure. Indeed this brutal separation from his life-sustaining source gives the child the impression that, in this situation of total vulnerability, someone is directly trying to snuff him out. He then goes through a powerful experience of being assaulted, which will easily reactivate old memories where an outside authority held sway over his life. **An active memory involving assault and powerlessness is then created**, which is all the more powerful as the physical body is itself in a state of panic regarding its own survival. In this state of panic, the child's instinct for self-preservation is turned on maximum. The body compensates by beginning to breathe immediately, without having had the time to get the lungs used to breathing. This has very negative consequences on every level, whether physical, emotional or mental.[4] As was the case with the two previous structures, the time of stress experienced at the time when the umbilical cord is severed is aggravated by cold, intense light, noise, as well as practices such as hanging the baby by his feet, slapping his bottom, cleaning him up, putting drops in his eyes, handling him and taking him away to a crib, all of which are perceived as physical assaults. Added to what we have already said about how the schizoid and oral structures are reactivated, is the experience of powerlessness and abuse of power, which generate the masochist structure. One can readily imagine all the past life situations that can be reactivated by such sensations. Such practices are sometimes essential in order to save the life of the baby, and there is no alternative but to impose these on him. But as much as possible, we should do our very best to avoid them. They are, in fact, used less and less these days, and more and more doctors, midwives and parents now try to work together so as to bring children into the world in a more conscious manner, based in some form or other on the principles of the Leboyer method.[5] This approach is very safe, and it affords the child a completely different welcome into a world of goodness, caring, gentleness and respect.

> This instant of birth, learn to respect it.
> Such a fragile moment, a subtle, evanescent movement as is each morning's awakening.
> One is in between two worlds, on a threshold.
> Wait, wait, let the birth take its time, in all its momentous gravity.
> This child is waking for the first time.
> Do not upset him in any way as he leaves the kingdom of dreams.
> See, one foot is running still, dwelling yet in the garden of his dream,
> as the other knocks against the edge of the bed!
> We have leaped into the world of time, out of eternity.
> This child has begun to breathe![6]

Children who were born through more conscious birthing methods have a concrete experience of being welcomed into a good, caring, gentle and respectful environment. Later on, they will turn out far more healthy, both mentally and physically. It has been observed that this approach produces self-confident teenagers and adults who have a trusting attitude towards life, who dare to come out of their shells, are much more open, generous and creative. These are people for whom the trauma of birth was reduced to a minimum, making it easier for them as adults to integrate harmoniously into the world, with good physical and moral health, springing from a far happier and calmer inner state.

But we must not lose sight of the fact that the child, as a soul, chooses his parents, and therefore the kind of birth he will experience. If there are traumas to be resolved, he will make sure that he experiences conditions during birth that are appropriate for that purpose. This does not mean that we should go on bringing children into the world in this manner. What has been done had to be done, for purposes of learning and evolution. No one is to blame, neither the parents, nor the doctors, nor anyone else. Each did his or her best with the awareness available at the time, and each of us is responsible for the experiences we create for ourselves. On the other hand, now that we are aware of the psychic dynamic in each child, we can choose to provide our children with less traumatic, and perhaps even healing conditions for their entry into life.

One good way to change the collective awareness would be to start with the first step, i.e. birth. Instead of bringing children into the world in a manner that is sure to reactivate violence and fear, we can allow them to have respect and love as an initial imprint into their memories by implementing new birthing methods. This could create a whole new generation of human beings.

> *If the new approach to childbirth leads to more sincerity, more respect for human life, more tenderness, then it will be a spiritual practice rather than just a birthing method. In the end, this Great Play is nothing but a bait to motivate us to review and correct our entire perception of worldly life.*[7]

• Early childhood

Generally speaking, children are obviously in a position of genuine physical powerlessness in relation to the adults around them.

Reich described this structure as developing between the ages of two and four. We feel that the experience of birth can also contribute to this development, but we have observed that this structure can, in fact, be reinforced even more specifically during this period of early childhood. This is indeed a period when memories related to self-expression and to powerlessness are likely to be reactivated.

First of all, any parent or adult can very easily dominate a child under a variety of pretexts. In particular, they will try to "educate" him, i.e. to force him to adopt a specific behaviour which he may or may not agree with. He is forced to eat, dress, go to the bathroom, and behave in certain ways that are not necessarily natural to him, and are often reinforced with punishments, threats or guilt. This can take the form of indirect psychological domination with emotional blackmail. In essence, the blackmailing goes something like this: "Behave in this manner, do what you are told, otherwise we withdraw our love". Or it can take the form of more direct assaults: children may be sexually abused, beaten, subjected to verbal or physical abuse, to varying degrees going from one extreme to another. As we have observed, indirect domination is not necessarily less damaging than direct assaults.

This is also a time when a child becomes far more self-aware and wants to be independent. He walks, talks, wants to act, take initiatives. But this is not always welcomed by the people around him. This stifling process is even more evident with regard to his freedom to act. Memories are all the more deeply reactivated as there is generally a karmic link between parents and children.

Little Johnny is four years old. A month ago, he saw his mother take great care to bake this wonderful cake for his grandmother's birthday. There was a family gathering, everyone was happy and the cake was greeted with great joy by all. Today, Johnny is home alone for the afternoon, with his babysitter who spends her time watching TV. His mother is having some important people over as guests this evening, including several colleagues from work, and she has spruced up the house for this reception. Suddenly, Johnny has this great idea: what if he baked a cake like the one he saw his mother make? That would be his contribution, and everyone would surely be very happy. So he gets to work, all excited, gets the ingredients from the cupboards, and begins to try different mixes. He gets more and more involved in this creative project, and the kitchen, from being spotlessly clean, soon turns into something like a war zone. His mother, who had gone out to get a few last minute things, comes home some time later. She smells something burning in the house, and heads for the kitchen. There is Johnny, all proud of himself, as his latest creation is in the oven and he feels sure that this is going to be a great surprise. But things don't quite turn out the way he had expected. When his mother sees the mess, the confusion in her kitchen and the disaster in the oven, she becomes very angry. She scolds Johnny in very stern words, heaping epithets on him and promising dire punishment. The babysitter, who had been sleeping in front of the TV set, wakes up and, feeling guilty, adds her own two cents worth: Johnny is stupid and his behaviour is intolerable, you just can't trust him for a moment, etc. Johnny ends up being sent to his room, where he is to stay for the rest of the day. There, behind the closed door, he suffers in total misery. His little heart, his love, his desire to create and to participate has been scorned. He is in pain and very angry at what he feels is an unjust fate. But human beings don't like to feel pain. So a very simple defence mechanism kicks in, which generalises according to the principle already described: "It is dangerous to express oneself, to try to freely create on one's own. There are powerful people who may disapprove, and that hurts." If Johnny has a few past memories that resonate with this experience, that is all that is needed for him to block any creative drive, and to develop an automatic fear reaction towards authority, a state of submission to the established order, in a general context of sadness and repressed anger against all these people who don't give him a chance to play and to create in uninhibited ways. Or, if he carries memories of a different type, the defence system may develop as a state of rebellion built on that same backdrop of inner protest but in a more externalised form.

There is no need for parents to be bad people for such reactivation to occur in a child. The least little act that he interprets as restricting his freedom can be a factor for reactivation if there is an underlying emotionally charged memory. If, for example, a child wants to run across a very busy street because a friend is calling him on the other side, and his mother prevents him from doing so, he may choose to interpret that as abuse of power. One must remember that the unconscious is not concerned with an intelligent perception of reality, but with an interpretation of reality based on its projected memories.

For this reason, it is very important not to get caught up in blame or guilt-wielding towards a so-called dysfunctional parent. And, except in cases involving directly violent or aggressive behaviour, parents are simply doing their best and are not responsible for the traumas of their children. Even violent parents are not to blame, since to some extent they too are doing their best on the basis of their own unconscious wounds. Parents need to heal the many hurts they carry within themselves and that cause them to act the way they do. Blame will not resolve anything. This principle should not, on the other hand, be used as a pretext to raise our children any old way, far from it (see *The Power of Free Will*).

Paul's arrival into this world was somewhat accidental. His was a very difficult birth: his mother suffered a great deal and so did he (a very lengthy birth process, forceps, etc.). He was a first child, and remained the only one. His parents' marriage was not the best, and after he came into the picture, his mother used him as a form of emotional compensation and focused all her attention on him. She doted on him to excess, while neglecting her husband more and more. The husband did not appreciate this at all. This situation, of course, was largely unspoken, but it translated into a domineering attitude on the part of his mother, and an unconscious resentment on the part of the father towards this son who had, in short, taken his wife away from him. The father's attitude thus became more and more distant and authoritarian. The family lived in a tiny house, with only one bedroom. Paul had to sleep on a sofa in the living room. His mother was a stickler for impeccability, and everything always had to be perfectly clean and tidy. As soon as he opened his eyes in the morning, Paul had to get out of bed, fold the sofa, and nothing was to show of his presence. Toys were forbidden: where would he have put them? There was just no room. It was also forbidden to invite friends, since that would disturb and soil the house. In addition, his father wouldn't stand for any noise. He was asked, in fact, to make himself invisible. If his presence became the least bit obvious, his father would get angry.

Looking desperately for a place he could call his own, Paul had found a fairly large closet in the kitchen. Inside, from the ceiling halfway down to the floor, there were shelves where his mother stored various dry ingredients. The bottom was closed off by a curtain, and behind the curtain was a large bag of potatoes as well as the vacuum cleaner in its original box. Paul had made his home there. Sitting on the vacuum cleaner box, behind the curtain, he could put together little things he could play with. He loved to perform experiments with oil lamps and small electric motors. Space was very cramped, of course, so he could hardly move, but at least he had this tiny space to himself: this was his universe. He was sure his father wouldn't like that, and for this reason only went there when his parents weren't around. Nevertheless, one day, his father caught him off guard. He had a violent fit and brutally dragged Paul out of the closet, forbidding him to ever go back there. His mother added her bit, since this damaged the vacuum cleaner box and wrinkled the curtains. It was unacceptable. Paul was more and more cautious, yet continued to go to his closet, always with the fear of being discovered. This, of course, happened again, and his father's anger became more and more violent with each incident. Paul was subjected to beatings and punishments.

During the whole period when he had to disappear from the living room from the moment he woke up in the morning, when he had to try not to exist so as not to disturb anyone or anything, when he was forbidden everything down to the tiny universe he had managed to create for himself under such difficult conditions, during all that time, Paul suffered in his heart, stifled by parental authority. As it always does, this suffering ended up generating within him a seething cauldron of anger towards his father's authority and his mother's smothering, which denied him his right to his own space, subjected him to daily put-downs, prevented him from playing, creating, or expressing himself, prevented him from living.

Years went by, and Paul stopped going to his closet. He developed a habit of living more and more outside of the family home, for what was there to come home to? He became detached from his parents, became self-supporting at a very early age, and all the pain and suffering of his childhood were stored away in his unconscious, but were all the more active in determining his choices and his reactions to the world around him.

As an adult, Paul is very sensitive to any form of authority. Following the mechanism described in Chapter 4 of *Free Your True Self 2*, he constantly projects his anger against anyone or anything that might represent an authority figure. He is incapable of working under anyone's "orders". For this reason, he decided to start his own business. But he ended up being a hateful boss. Perpetually unsatisfied, ready to get angry at the least little problem, always wanting to be right, constantly judging and condemning his employees, demanding more, in short behaving in an authoritarian manner exactly as his father had done with him. The same holds true of his personal relationships. He easily becomes demanding, aggressive, often mean and nasty. Afterwards, he wonders how he could react this way. But he just can't figure it out, saying he "can't help it", and he remains caught in this mechanism which ruins both his personal and his professional relationships. As an outlet for this repressed anger, he has developed an acid sense of humour that often gets people laughing, but can also cut very deeply. Paul does not hurt people deliberately, as he is basically a good man. But his behaviour is automatic. The unexpressed rage and aggressiveness he felt as a child are always ready to come to the surface. Expressing this rage and aggressiveness doesn't help matters, on the contrary. On the one hand, it ruins any relationship he may have, and Paul then finds himself rejected as he was in childhood (he then reinforces his masochistic belief system: "People are stupid and mean, no one has any sense of the great heart beating in me"; he thus validates his programming); on the other hand, the more he expresses this anger, the more he feeds it, since by expressing it he keeps replaying the mechanism, and thus maintaining it.

Paul is caught in an active masochist structure. Only through awareness of the mechanism and sustained work aimed at defusing the memories will he be able to rediscover himself, to develop a more accurate perception of reality in the here and now, and to generate love and support around him instead of animosity. For as we know, when we behave aggressively (consciously or unconsciously) with the people around us, this reactivates their own aggressiveness (unless they happen to be very evolved beings who control their emotions). We then get an escalation of violence, whether in direct or indirect form.

Those family living conditions fostered the development of the masochist structure in Paul, as well as the fourth structure which we will describe in the following chapter.

Children react at a very early age to this kind of stifling situation, which is not always as evident as in Paul's case, yet is no less damaging. They rebel against restrictions imposed on them in the past and in the present, and they do this with whatever means are available to them: whims, tantrums, resistance, the "no" phase, etc. We see this as normal because it is common. Yet it is only common because we are programmed in a more or less similar manner, and we subject our children to somewhat the same fate. In fact, this is not normal. Generally speaking, instead of paying attention to this resistance, and finding original and loving ways to deal with it, parents resist and react by stifling the child even more, forbidding him to behave this way, making him feel guilty and demanding that he repress any anger or protest; which is what children generally end up doing. They make themselves scarce. This will produce masochist structures that are deeply rooted in the unconscious, and that will determine highly inadequate behaviour later on, when the child becomes an adult. Once again, it is pointless to blame one's parents. We are describing an interaction between mechanisms, that of the parents who were once children, and that of the children, who will one day be parents. Mechanisms are just mechanisms: they do not define a person.

• Notes for parents

We can hear the protests of parents, saying: "But really, I can't let my child do whatever he wants to do, any way he feels like doing it! I have to show him how to behave: that's my role as a parent!" This is quite true. But it is very important to give a fair amount of thought to what exactly is the role of a parent, so as not to unconsciously repeat what our parents did with us.

To help clarify our behaviour with our children, we can ask ourselves this question, for example: what I am trying to "teach" my children, is it really important for the sake of fulfilling their creativity, their soul qualities and their freedom? Is it necessary in order to foster their respect for the environment and for others, so that they learn mastery of their world? Or is it rather a set of ready-made ideas I hold as the "right" way to act in life, ideas that may stem from my past programmings and my own childhood experiences, which often remained unintegrated?

This questioning attitude is not an easy one to adopt. When parents ask us what they can do for their children, we strongly suggest that they do some inner work aimed at defusing their own memories. For children essentially learn by "modelling" themselves according to their perception of their parents. They do not model themselves strictly on what is consciously evident, far from it. In fact, they resonate a lot more deeply with the unconscious part of their parents. Our children have their own past and their own personal level of evolution. But they also at least partly mirror what is carried in our unconscious. Looking at things from this viewpoint is very helpful in getting to know oneself

Doing inner work aimed at unjamming the mechanism of our unconscious is the greatest service we can render our children. They benefit directly from this work. We have heard a great number of testimonials from children whose behaviour changed radically after their parents, especially the mother, did some inner liberating work.

As an example, we have the mother of a four-year-old little girl named Abbie. Every morning, Abbie would have a fit when it came time to get her dressed. It was a real chore. Her mother took part in one of my workshops, and forgot about her daughter's behaviour. She was quite satisfied with the inner work she did, especially in relation to her own mother. At no point was there any reference to her daughter or to any particular philosophy on how to conduct oneself with one's children. Back home, Monday morning, she expected the usual tantrum. What a surprise to find that her daughter was willing to get dressed without difficulty. She thought this was some sort of coincidence. But the next day, again, there was no tantrum, nor were there any tantrums in the following days. Abbie never again threw fits over getting dressed in the morning

One could talk about coincidence if this were an isolated case. But we have heard about so many "coincidences" of this type that it is impossible not to admit that whatever inner work parents do has a deep resonance with their children.[8]

The most effective general attitude to have is to approach a child with great respect, love, understanding, compassion, and active listening, **from the moment of birth** (and even before that). We know that an infant is aware and very sensitive, carrying all of his past experiences, that he will have to find the way to his soul through the trials and tribulations of life. If we know how to listen, to be sensitive to his needs, he will tell us what he really needs; we will hear him and will be able to respond appropriately. Feeling respected, he will more willingly accept the restrictions of physical life that we suggest, intuitively understanding that this is not abuse of power, but rather a form of parental support. We can then give him a flexible and effective framework in which to grow as he really is, in all of his original beauty. This attitude will not remove the personal memories that the child has chosen to work on, nor will it prevent these memories from being reactivated, or the child from going through certain experiences of his own choosing. But he will have support along the way, and this is what any parent can aspire to become.

It is also worth remembering that, according to our model, if it is true that a child chooses his parents, it is also true that parents choose a particular child. This choice is made at the level of the soul, through energetic attraction, on the basis of all previously established karmic links and the work to be done in order to proceed along the path of evolution. This choice is obviously not made at the personality level. Our Self sends us these children in order to help us grow, to educate us.

Beyond the parents' influence, as he grows up, a child will have more and more opportunities to be in contact with other people who have more power than him. Particularly in school, teachers and other bigger or stronger students, if only physically, will create numerous circumstances fostering abuse of power, in subtle or coarse form. In our society, where lack of awareness is still rampant, a child will have all he needs to reactivate this type of memory and redevelop a passive or aggressive victim structure for the rest of his life.

• Adolescence

During adolescence, we will find a natural process of rebellion against this whole dynamic. At that point, an individual feels much less dependent on his parents or other people, and he can afford to let his anger explode, along with his protests against the stifling influence he has experienced. This is a very healthy process, which should be supported and monitored, rather than stifled by a society that has a hard time accepting individuality and personal freedom. Even if the parents had been "perfect", this period of teenage rebellion has to be lived. This is indeed the time when a child naturally takes leave of his parents' space, of their influence, in order to try to define his own individuality, his originality, to define himself as a free and self-reliant being. He has to go through a period of rejection of everything around him so that he can come back to it later on in a free and creative manner. This is a pendulum phenomenon, excess in one direction; followed by excess in the other, in order to eventually find a balance. Healthy rebellion is quite a good thing during adolescence. And nothing is more unsettling than an overly docile teenager, for this can mean that he is afraid of living this rebellion, and that he is repressing rage and guilt which, unfortunately, may strongly condition his adult behaviour later on.

All of these conditions, affecting past lives, birth, and childhood, are generally found to be the source of the development of a masochist defence system, which we shall now describe more specifically.

5-4   The Masochist Structure's Defence System

> ✓ **The underlying fear of structure:** fear of being stifled, fear of power, fear of being taken, fear of being manipulated and exploited.
>
> ✓ **Emotional charge:** sense of powerlessness, anger, rage, resentment, jealousy, sense of injustice.
>
> ✓ **Basic defence system:** submission, rebellion, criticism, sabotage, blame, negativity, complaints, agressivity, guilt.
>
> ✓ **Statement of this structure:**
>
>
>
> "LIFE IS PAINFUL AND UNFAIR, POOR ME!
> People are mean, I am powerless".
>
>

To this statement, the following could be added:

> **It's other people's fault!**
> Why me?
> **Look out: they're here to put one over me**; be careful!
> **Down with power** (my own as well as other people's)!
> I'm right, others are wrong.
> **I suffer** because of other people.
> People don't respect me.
> Life is unfair, but some day **I'll get even**!
> I've given too much and haven't received enough.

5-5 Typical Behaviours of the Masochist Structure

1) General attitude towards life

The masochist structure wrestles with the problem of power. In this structure, one nurtures a permanent deep sense of **powerlessness**. This sense is so deeply buried that, in most cases, one is not able to recognise it. Yet, according to the dynamics of the lower mind, one constantly projects all the **abuses of power we have been subjected to** on present situations. One is unable to see reality as it is and one interprets it on the basis of one's memories.

Thus one manages to make life difficult for oneself so as to justify one's inner anger and frustration. Whatever the circumstances, we will always find something that prevents us from doing what we want to do, being who we want to be, something that isn't going right. As the active memories are loaded with repressed complaints, protests and suffering, one must find reasons to continue to complain; if obvious reasons are lacking, one invents them.

In *The Power of Free Will*, in the chapter entitled "The Symptoms of Victimitis", I offered a detailed description of the victim's behaviours which, in fact, stems from a non-transformed masochist structure. Let us briefly restate the following characteristics:

—Life is perceived as a constant battle, a losing one at that, all because of other people.

—The **fear of being taken** is deeply ingrained. **Mistrust** is always there, combined with rage and anger, constantly idling. One always suspects others are trying to take advantage.

—The **fear of authority and resistance to authority**, or to anything that looks like it, fosters a permanent state of stress.

—One's life is poisoned by **jealousy** towards everyone who looks happy.

—**Criticism and put-downs**, sabotage in direct or subtle form, practised abundantly, feed negativity and frustration.

—**One suffers** and lives unhappily so as to justify one's memories.

—One's basic feeling of frustration leads to a permanent attitude of **ill will**.

—**One RESISTS life**, no matter the circumstances. **EVERYTHING IS GOING WRONG...** but it's all other people's fault, so...

—**One likes to blame.** Indeed not only does one complain, but one also blames others. This unconscious discontent is constantly being projected on everything: one's spouse, children, friends, colleagues at work, one's boss or employees, society, business people or clients, God, the weather, the neighbour's dog, anything, just as long as one has something to complain about, criticise, and make someone or something responsible for one's troubles.

To illustrate this attitude, here is an extract from a newspaper article:[9]

IT'S NOT ME, IT'S HIM

You've had it with winter and don't know what to do with your days to forget the bad weather? Here's an idea for you: play the victim. It's funny, entertaining, and, with a measure of stubbornness and originality on your part, it can even make you a bundle of cash.

The point of the game is simple: you want to make as many people as possible shed tears over your burden of woes. You find yourself a scapegoat, and you make him or her responsible for everything that's happening to you, and you whimper alone in your little corner until the media show up. The first player who gets invited to the UN gets the jackpot.

Few games have reached this level of popularity. Look around you: today, everyone plays the victim.

- *Women claim to be victims of men, who abuse them.*
- *Men claim to be victims of women, who castrate them. [...]*
- *Politicians claim to be victims of the media, who badmouth them.*
- *The media claim to be victims of the public, who accuse them of being biased.*
- *Blacks claim to be victims of the police, who fire at them on sight.*
- *Police officers claim to be victims of Blacks, who call them racist.*
- *Creative artists claim to be victims of critics, who scrap their work.*
- *Critics claim to be victims of producers, who despise them.*
- *Workers claim to be victims of employers, who exploit them.*
- *Employers claim to be victims of workers,who drive them to bankrupcy.[...]*
- *Citizens claim to be victims of the State, that overtaxes them.*
- *The State claims to be the victim of citizens, who shop in the U.S.*
- *Non-smokers claim to be victims of smokers, who foul the air they breathe.*
- *Smokers claim to be victims of non-smokers, who bully them.*
- *Etc., etc.*

Everywhere you get this same litany of victims and perpetrators, as if dialogue had suddenly become impossible and we didn't know any better than to point fingers after washing our hands of everything.

What is weird about all this victim talk is that it recognises the omnipotence of the perpetrators. Indeed if the perpetrators are solely responsible for our problems, they are the only ones who can bring an end to our misery.

"We have become a nation of wimps", we read on the title page of Time magazine some months ago. We sue each other like crazy, we denounce each other before the cameras, we condemn each other. We live in the great Quarrel era. [...]

Now even politicians have taken to victim talk. These days, if you want to get elected, you don't come up with a program, no: you just focus on destroying your opponent's. "Mr. So-&-So is corrupt; Mrs. What's-her-Name is incompetent. So vote for me!" [...]

If this keeps up, we'll end up creating a veritable victim culture. A bitter culture, steeped in worry and anger, that will explode in an orgy of rage and recriminations. It will be nobody's fault, and it will be everybody's fault.

Everybody will be lily white, everybody will be black as night, and everybody will accuse everybody. After years of wrangling, we will finally all be on an equal footing. All the same, all similar, all victims.

This text, taken from a popular cultural journal, shows the extent to which this dynamic is rooted in the collective consciousness.

The masochist structure constantly feeds fear and anger. If fear is the predominant emotion, anger is deeply repressed and we get what is called a "passive masochist". If it's anger, we get behaviours associated with an "active masochist". Thus we will find two types of defence systems, with every possible variation and degree in between:

- **The passive masochist's defence system: submission**

This defence system is based on fear of being stifled and of suffering further pain. In our cultural conditioning, this aspect is more often found in women. The individual suffers in silence because she is much too afraid of expressing or manifesting herself (this is what led to past bullying), but it is often a silence that speaks loudly. In the presence of any form of authority, or whatever looks like it, it is better to bow and to submit rather than risk the pain one has experienced (passive victim who gets into indirect sabotage, who self destructs, which can also be a devious means of destroying others). The anger is there, but deeply repressed.

- **The active masochist's defence system: rebellion**

This defence system is based on anger and aggressiveness, on unconscious projections of accumulated anger on all those who have bullied him in the past, an anger which he directly, and sometimes violently expresses over everything and anything. It's always other people's fault, and he is going to let them know about it. This is the dynamic that will lead, sooner or later, to acts of revenge and direct sabotage. This can turn a victim into a very violent person, or even a perpetrator (aggressive victim who destroys others). The fear is still there, but deeply repressed.

2) Relationships
• **Couple relationships:**   STIFLED HEART

"Life is tough, I am suffering (because of you)."

Since the dynamic of the masochist structure is to make life difficult, when an individual feels like a prisoner, he will tend to be drawn into a relationship with a perpetrator. This can be a genuine perpetrator, i.e. someone who behaves in mean or violent ways, or a "false" perpetrator, i.e. someone who behaves in ordinary ways, but on whom he will project all his complaints and expectations in order to be able to suffer and to blame. Generally speaking, in this structure, we accuse others of bullying us, abusing us, causing us harm, preventing us from living.

One thus projects those memories of exploitation and abuse onto one's partner, with all that inwardly accumulated aggressiveness, frustration and resentment, whether expressed or repressed. Any minor action on the other's part is blown out of proportion in order to prove how much he makes us unhappy, and how right we are. One plays the card of **heroism and sacrifice**, as one is definitely a wonderful person, while the other is selfish, ungrateful, hard, etc. In a couple relationship, the masochist's subtle or direct weapon is to **make the other feel guilty**.

"If I don't get to have power, then nobody gets to have power."

This dynamic where one makes the other feel at fault and ill at ease can be very subtle. In the context of a relationship, the masochist structure, which suffers from having lost contact with its own power, will behave either openly or very subtly in such a way as to make sure the other also has no power. Masochists are often sick, that way they have good reason to suffer. Furthermore, it is also a very good way to force the other to care for this poor suffering being, and thus to siphon the other's energy. If the partner is the saviour type (such as found in the masochist and the psychopath structures), he will play up to this for a while, up to the point when it becomes intolerable. At that point, he will get mad, and probably quit the relationship. The poor victim will find herself not only sick but also alone. What a dire fate! And this game will go on until it attracts another person who is also caught in his or her own mechanisms, and thus the masochist structure takes power away from everybody. This is its basic dynamic: since I don't have any power, nobody will have power, and since I get no pleasure out of life, nobody is entitled to have any either.

More specifically, in the **passive masochist structure** rooted in fear, we find the following behaviours in the context of relationships:

—**Submission**, obedience, niceness, passivity. The individual deeply represses his anger. In a conflict, he will lock himself up in silence and heroic suffering. If he also has a schizoid structure, it will be easy for him to disappear in his own suffering. He will eventually face the conflict through subtle sabotage.

—He is so afraid of expressing himself sincerely that he will deny his own needs instead of letting them be known, so as to be able to complain to the other later on in indirect ways that she didn't do anything to meet them, and thus continue to suffer. He does not communicate his frustration either, and plays the **martyr**.

—**No matter what the other does**, he feels poor, unhappy, abandoned, unloved, stifled, and sad.

—The other has no right to be happy (with or without him), as this is an insult to his suffering.

—**Manipulates through meekness** and niceness, camouflaging a time bomb of repressed anger and resentment, **and through guilt**.

—A masochist of this type will generally choose a partner of the two following types of structure (psychopath or rigid) often combined with an oral structure, which makes them experts in possession and domination: perfect "perpetrators".

As far as the **active masochist structure** is concerned, we find the following characteristics:

—Permanent **discontent** and openly expressed moodiness. Dissatisfaction here is based on anger (rather than on deprivation, as in the case of the oral structure). If the masochist structure is combined with an oral structure, we get someone who is very deeply frustrated, constantly in a state of deprivation and anger (it's no fun).

—**Projection of anger** on the partner in the form of blame, criticism and direct complaints.

—**Feels dominated, manipulated** by the other; complains that the other prevents him from living his life and doesn't respect him.

—Lets loose his aggressiveness bit by bit, at carefully chosen moments, especially when the partner is vulnerable.

—**Manipulates through blame, criticism and complaints**, generally quite openly, in the hope that the other will feel guilty and or will end up changing. Even if the other changed and met every possible requirement, the dissatisfaction would remain, as **this is not about the other, but about a memory projected onto the other**.

—Deals with conflict through anger, complaints and blame.

—Can become very violent.

Let us note that the characteristics found in the context of couple relationships are no different from those found in the dynamics of general relationships with others (work colleagues, family, fellow service volunteers, friends). This description can thus be applied to all relationships, in addition to the general behaviours described earlier.

If the structure is really strong (active or passive) and overthrows the dynamics of the soul, the individual is incapable of loving, projecting his negativity, his frustration and his fears on everyone, especially those closest to him. In so doing, he often makes people impatient or aggressive, which only serves to reinforce the model according to which people are mean.

• Relationship with children

An individual who is caught in this structure will easily project his frustration and anger on weaker people, especially children. Victim parents easily become perpetrators. We know that often parents who were beaten as children will beat their own children. If it isn't physical **violence**, it will often take the form of verbal violence.

An individual of the passive masochist type will be very impatient with children's joy and vitality, which are an insult to his suffering. He will do everything to curb this vitality and lock children up in restrictions and taboos which mimic the stifling influence of his own experience.

The parent will make maximum use of **guilt** in order to manipulate his children. This will have very unfortunate consequences, as children are very sensitive to this kind of manipulation which quickly destroys any self-confidence they might have, and can often lead to self-doubt if they are not strong enough to counteract this influence.

• Working relationships

It is interesting to examine this aspect for this structure, as it is very sensitive to hierarchy. If the individual is an employee, one can easily imagine the attitudes he will have: apparent submission with rancour and anger against employers and colleagues, irresponsibility towards assigned work, or barely concealed rebellion. Both aspects generate a great deal of **resistance** to any assigned work, obviously with a reluctance to cooperate and find solutions that might work. Things just can't go smoothly.

If the individual is in a position of responsibility, he will do his best to make things difficult for those working under his supervision. No question of having any fun here. He will, of course, complain incessantly about the incompetence of those under his employ. He will be incapable of empowering his team, since he has lost his own power.

3) Sexuality

The dynamic of frustration will have an impact on sexual relationships which, by that very fact, will rarely be truly satisfactory. This structure generates so much stress and inner tension, and blocks the energy for pleasure to such an extent, that often the men are impotent and the women frigid. Sexual satisfaction requires letting go, surrendering and being open, and this becomes very difficult for such individuals. Frigidity in women often stems from this structure combined with the fifth (rigid), which we will examine further on. Finding simple pleasure in one's body runs counter to the masochist structure since life is supposed to be nothing but suffering.

The attitude can be somewhat different among active masochists. Sexual activity is often sought as a means of momentarily letting loose an excess of repressed energy or, more directly, as an opportunity to let out some aggressiveness and underhandedly actualise one's sense of domination and revenge. In such cases, the individual is very active sexually. But the sense of deep discontent remains, no matter what.

4) The physical body
• Body shape

The masochist memory says that one has been stifled and that one is heavily burdened. In such cases, it is not surprising to note that the person often has a slumped back, caved in chest, bowed head (passive masochist) or perked up in a provocative stance, chin forward on a slumped back (active masochist).

• Health

Being sick is of great interest to the masochist structure. When one is sick, one suffers; one has grounds for complaining and looking pathetic. This works very well in our highly victimised society. We force people to take care of us, and if they don't, we have even more reasons to complain and feel frustrated with people's ungratefulness.

We want to avoid being simplistic here, and argue that all sick people are systematically caught in this mechanism, for the psychological sources of illness are complex and varied. But it is very often the case. This is not a matter of blaming oneself or blaming individuals who are caught in this mechanism, thus losing any compassion for human suffering, on the contrary. Recognising the structure should allow us to get free of it, and thus to get well more quickly.

Apart from this interest of the unconscious for generating illness, all the accumulated emotional negativity obviously leads to a whole array of physical ailments.

—Rancour, resentment, and anger often affect the entire digestive tract, and generate an endless list of illness: **chronic liver malfunctions**,[10] stomach ulcers, intestinal blocks, insomnia, etc.

—Stress due to anger suppression generates **backaches, and strong tensions in the shoulders**. We may go to a chiropractor for years; the same symptoms keep coming back if the source is not dealt with. When inner work is done in conjunction with strictly physical treatment (whether physiotherapy, chiropractic treatments or other approaches), the latter becomes highly effective and durable. Otherwise the unconscious constantly recreates bodily tensions in accordance with the messages it seeks to convey: life is tough and

I am overburdened. As long as one remains programmed in this manner, any attempt at treatment from an external source will necessarily be of limited effectiveness or temporary.

—The deep sense of powerlessness generates a kind of unconscious hopelessness that manifests in the form of **anxiety and depression**. Depression is a typical illness for the masochist structure.

—One's inability to deal with joy blocks vitality. We then find cases of **chronic fatigue**, a lack of energy that opens the door to various common illnesses: influenza, colds, etc.

• Attitude towards food

Being sick frequently, often at the digestive level, an individual caught in the masochist structure will never be able to indulge in gastronomical excesses. In fact, he will make sure that all pleasures of the table are forbidden ground to him, so that life is even less amusing. He is resigned to this, but in the same way as he is resigned to other things, i.e. reinforcing his frustration with this life which is definitely no fun.

If there are no digestive problems, he will make sure he finds some strict nutritional theory that makes things that are good for you not very good to taste, or very time-consuming and difficult to prepare. In any case, this structure will make sure that food, like anything else in life, will be a source of difficulties rather than joy.

• Automatic choices in clothing

Since the idea is to be right by giving oneself reasons for suffering, the structure will generally lead to wearing uncomfortable clothes. This may seem ridiculous, yet this is what I have observed all too often for it to be just a matter of coincidence. Witness the example of Josie, a near caricature, yet true to life:

Josie, having a schizo-masochist structure, always had pains in her feet. This pain made her life really difficult. She had seen many specialists about this problem. Doctors gave her ointments to ease the pain; an osteopath gave her exercises to do to loosen her feet; an orthopaedist prescribed special shoes, but God were they ugly! And she would have liked to wear shoes like everyone else. She had even seen a medium who told her that if she had pains in her feet, it was because she was reluctant to move ahead in life. This was not unreasonable, but Josie was left with a vague sense of guilt (after all, it was her fault if she had pains in her feet). No matter what treatments or suggestions she followed, as soon as she wore nice looking "normal" shoes, the pain in her feet would resurface. Josie felt very powerless with this state of affairs. Nobody had thought to ask her what size shoes she wore. In fact, Josie had always bought shoes that were at least a half-size too small.

Stupid? Yes, but that is the way it is: traumas make us stupid, and not just when it comes to buying shoes.

In addition, as a schizo, Josie was always cold. On the other hand, as a true masochist, she never dressed adequately for winter. She could thus spend her time complaining about the weather and have good reasons both to suffer (the masochist in her) and to hate the physical world (the schizo). Many people had already drawn her attention to the fact that one can dress more warmly and be quite comfortable, even when it's cold outside. This had all started with her parents, but curiously Josie had never really heard the message. Her unconscious blocked the information so that it could continue to control her behaviour and make her choose clothes on the basis of her programming according to which life is tough. It is interesting to note also that when Josie did some inner liberation work, it became quite natural for her to buy shoes of the right size and to wear warmer clothes. She stopped forgetting her sweaters at home.

This may seem ridiculously simple. Though we may be rich and complex at the level of the soul, the mechanisms of the lower mind, on the other hand, are quite primary. This actual example is a good illustration of the way this mechanism works. This was about clothes, which may seem minor and may not be our problem. But we must see that **many of our choices, whether important or not, are conditioned by the same dynamic, and are dependent on our structures and on the defence system that is active within us**. This is not rational or intelligent. But we all function this way, and it is better to acknowledge this if we want to have any chance of recovering some measure of freedom. **We can begin to be truly intelligent and free only when our unconscious mental-emotional mechanisms are no longer operative**.

5) The energy aspect

A masochist is heavily drawn into himself and his pain, and does not radiate. In fact, his energy is heavily compacted inside of him.[11]

In the presence of a masochist structure, one feels ill at ease, without really knowing why, and one quickly feels exhausted. In fact, the individual is always energetically oozing the message of the victim: "Poor me, I am suffering, and If I'm suffering, it is other people's fault, i.e. yours." Being always ready to find fault with other people, the masochist's energy tends to make others feel "not ok", and ultimately guilty.

A masochist can be capable of great endurance, even though he may often be sick or physically weak. Behind these apparent physical weaknesses lay hidden all the power and energy of repressed anger. Even though he may feel tired because of energy blockage, he can find an enormous amount of energy all at once if he finds an outlet for his aggression. Under this fragile appearance, a masochist individual is, in fact, very strong and has a lot of available energy.

6) Relating to the material world and money

Since a strong masochist structure always manages to make life difficult, it will have a great deal of trouble generating abundance. The more financially strapped the individual is, the more he has good reason to complain, to be stressed out and afraid. The masochist structure usually leads to poverty. And even if the individual happens to be well off, he will somehow suffer as a result of his wealth, living in fear of being exploited, since "people are mean", and he will, of course, be very wary of being taken in.

A masochist will manage to either fail in his material endeavours or make them very difficult. Furthermore, because of its latent sense of injustice, this structure will tend to be envious of others, especially those who are materially comfortable. He will even suspect them of all manner of wrongdoing. At the level of the unconscious, being happy and prosperous is almost an insult. This negative attitude certainly does not foster the creation of wealth and success.

7) Relating to power

Relating to power is the primary difficulty with this structure, and one outcome of this difficulty is **resistance to power**.

The "submission-rebellion" dynamic (denial of one's own power–fear, or resistance towards other people's power–anger) is in high gear in this area. This is the key feature of this structure, and it generates very strong reactions towards power.

Let us note that, as there is obviously no power or freedom in submission, neither is there any power in rebellion. When we rebel, we don't do what we want: we simply do the contrary of what others want. So our actions are still based on outside influence rather than on our own free will, regardless of other people's input. Sometimes, of course, on the way to self-transformation, after an extended period of submission, we may need to go through an intermediate phase of rebellion in order to find our way back to our own power. But this phase has to be temporary if we want to gain genuine independence later on.

When we are caught in a masochist structure, **we hate power, our own** (because of our past experiences as perpetrators) **and other people's** (because of our past experiences as victims). Therefore we will not seek power directly; instead **we will struggle against power**. A masochist will live in constant reaction against authority, which he will blindly project on everything and anything. It is sometimes perfectly appropriate to fight off certain forms of power. But in the case of masochists, this kind of discernment is non-existent. The motivation to fight against power, in any form, is not an objective or intelligent motivation; rather it is a traumatic, therefore blind and by that very fact largely ineffectual motivation. **The violence that masochists struggle against is just a mirror of the violence they carry within themselves**. This struggle, therefore, can only generate more violence.

We have observed that masochists often share one particular dynamic, that is commonly found in people assuming a saviour role. Indeed, protecting poor victims is an outlet for their own rage against this world that causes "the innocent" to suffer. Unfortunately, they will be unable to hand back their power to the victims they "save", since they have lost contact with their own power. On the contrary, they will keep feeding the victims with rancour and anger against the bad people who abused them, and nurturing their sense of powerlessness, which will only dig them deeper into the root cause of their suffering.

A masochist perceives others according to three categories:

✓ the victims he wants to save;

✓ the perpetrators, the bad people, the ungrateful and the disrespectful punks he wants to destroy;

✓ the idols on whom he projects his ideals, but whom he will generally, sooner or later, relegate back to the "perpetrator" category (no matter what the quality of the idealised person may be), when the mechanism of criticism and aggression takes over once again.

Seeing the world as split in two, the poor defenceless victims and the fat perpetrators, the individual who is caught in this structure is incapable of helping someone find his or her power. On the contrary, since the sense of powerlessness is deeply rooted in his consciousness, he will inevitably take away power from everyone around him, no matter what he does.

8) Work

An individual caught in this structure will rarely be happy in his job, where he will project a lot of frustrations which he will not share with anyone. Communicating might help to make things better, and, unconsciously, he wants things to continue just the way they are so as to be able to complain and nurture bad feelings towards everybody. Even in ideal working conditions, he will always find a reason to be dissatisfied and frustrated. He is incapable of seeing the good side of things, and refuses to change his perspective, since this might make the situation less unpleasant, and then he would no longer have any reason to bitch and complain. Passive masochists will rarely be in positions of leadership. They will generally manage to work under someone else's orders so as to have real or imagined reasons to feel stifled by a higher power. Active masochists may have their own businesses. They will then manage to complain about unfavourable circumstances beyond their control. They will choose a demanding profession, where one must work long hours, often in relation to a demanding clientele or in a high pressure environment, so that they can run themselves ragged at work and whine. On the other hand, they will have an astonishing capacity to hang on, as this structure can store up a great deal of energy and is able to "take a lot of hard knocks".

9) Service

In this structure, service will be reclaimed, just like everything else, to justify defence systems. Masochists will thus often be found in situations that foster a saviour role. As we mentioned earlier, this allows them either to play the heroic martyr, or to feed their rage and anger against the entire world. They will there-fore often be involved with charitable organisations, working zealously, even fanatically, to the point of self-sacrifice, in order to come to the aid of these poor victims of other people's meanness. The individual desperately seeks to heal the suffering he carries within himself. Unfortunately, this doesn't work for those who are being helped and who need to be exposed to a radiant, unadulterated energy of love that can help them reclaim their own power; and it doesn't work for the individual himself, as this only serves to reinforce the structure in which he remains caught.

The "sacrifice-martyr" attitude will lead masochists to seek care-giving occupa-tions. Nursing is a good place to exercise self-sacrifice and at the same time to experience powerlessness in relation to the power of doctors. Of course, many people who take on such positions can be very courageous and generous indi-viduals whose dedication springs from the energy of the soul, and who are happy to make their contribution in this profession. But if the ego reclaims this situation, as in many other similar cases, then the individual can easily take on an attitude of sacrifice-service, and activate all the mechanisms of powerlessness and victimhood.

10) Pitfalls in spiritual seeking

The basic attitude inherent in this structure is a major handicap for spiritual development. **The belief that one is powerless, that life is unfair and subject to chance, and that every setback is always someone else's fault, amounts to closing the door on the power of one's soul.**

If a personal development process or a process of spiritual inquiry is undertak-en while this structure remains active or unrecognised, the ego can reclaim every-thing to its own advantage. For example, masochists will generally choose fairly emotional and difficult paths that require a great deal of effort. They might be involved in harrowing personal development workshops, or choose very demanding spiritual disciplines (preferably with a guru, so that this authority fig-ure can become an object of loathing later on) where they will invest all of their belongings and will apparently give the shirt off their backs without expectations (appearances can be deceiving) in a rush of excessive submission-devotion. They will then be in a better position to stumble back into a state of frustration, criti-cism and denigration, and to feel they have been taken in (the submission-rebel-lion dynamic common to masochists). That will serve as fodder for their bitter-ness and resentment for years, even as they work to recreate the same dynamic somewhere else, which all amounts to blocking any chance for genuine inner work.

11) Some practical suggestions and tasks leading to transformation

To get free of this structure, one must reconnect with one's true source of power, i.e. the soul. For this to take place, it will be necessary to focus a great deal of work on healing past wounds set deeply in the unconscious, and thus liberate oneself from anger and the sense of injustice. One will then be able to straighten one's back and become more open to life and to love.

One can start working on this structure at a conscious level. The first attitude that has to go is that of the victim. The principle of "responsibility-attraction-creation", as described in *The Power of Free Will*, is one way to free oneself specifically from this dynamic and to reconnect with one's creative power, by recognising the fact that one is the source of one's evolutionary process. Once it is fully understood, it gives that power back to us, along with the capacity to create a free and satisfying life. It is a fundamental key that opens the door to transformation.

> The principle of **responsibility-attraction-creation** offers a way to defuse the masochist structure on a conscious level, and to reconnect with the power of the soul.

To support the transformation of this structure in our daily existence, we can practice the following disciplines:

—apply the principle of responsibility-attraction-creation in every event of our existence, from the most insignificant to the most important;

—begin to **take responsibility** for our emotional reactions;

—**stop complaining**, judging and blaming others (this is already quite a program!);

—**stop criticising** (when criticism is about to roll off the tongue, turn it into a heavy sigh, then into a burst of laughter);

—stop dramatising and cultivate humour;

—play like a child, either with children or with adults, laugh a lot;

—take care of ourselves and treat ourselves to small and major pleasures: sensual massage, candlelight dinners;

—get into physical exercise in order to liberate the energy blocked by anger;

—stop creating suffering for ourselves in order to be right; be gentle and kind to ourselves;

—watch a funny movie at least once a month;

—consciously choose to see the glass as being half-full instead of half-empty;

—cultivate an attitude of **contentment and gratitude in all circumstances**;

—practice **GOOD WILL**, one of the most beautiful qualities of the soul; along with the principle of responsibility-attraction-creation, it is the most potent antidote to victimitis;

—relearn to accept others as they are, and to love life.

It is easy to see how deeply entrenched this structure is in the collective unconscious, and how it conditions the behaviour of most people, with all the suffering and limitations this implies.

Victmitis is a planetary plague that must be brought to light and confronted if humanity is ever to recover a genuine state of power and freedom. It can be dispelled through the transformation of consciousness.

> *Liberating this structure within mankind would bring great changes in all aspects of society, i.e. economics, politics, as well as social and cultural life.*[12]

Yet, however limiting this structure may appear, let us remember that our experience of life through such mechanisms is never lost, far from it. Despite the pain and difficulties encountered, whether personal or collective, and in fact because of these, a whole process of maturation of the personality is taking place. At one point, it becomes sufficiently developed and flexible to let the light and the will of the soul shine through a totality of fluid structures that are enriched with the experiences encountered through the millennia.

What do all these experiences as victims and perpetrators spread over thousands of years lead to, once all that baggage has been transcended?

5-6 The Masochist Structure Transformed

> *Just as conserved heat is transmuted into energy,*
> *thus our controlled anger can be transmuted*
> *into a power that can move the world.*
> —*Mahatma Gandhi*

• **Qualities**

First of all, these experiences have led to the development of **compassion**. Indeed, one has truly learned the meaning of suffering, and thus one becomes very sensitive and attentive to global suffering. The heart has become compassionate and **generous**.

In addition, masochists have been able to endure many things, and to shoulder great burdens. This structure, once transformed, leads to **toughness** (you can count on him) and **reliability**. It also leads to enormous **endurance** at all levels, and unfailing **courage**, springing from the heart. One becomes capable of working tirelessly for long hours, if it can help someone.

Once transformed, masochists become eminently supportive and devoted. Having recovered the true power of the soul, they are able to support others so that they too can find their own power and their ability to make a difference. They can be excellent coaches and teachers.

They naturally become very respectful towards everyone's autonomy. Having transcended memories of abuse, they really know what respect for others is all about, and it is now deeply rooted in their consciousness. They will always honour the trust that others place in them, and respect will always be a priority.

Service and self-sacrifice become natural sources of joy and inspiration. While, in its non-transformed stage, the structure led to one's participation in charitable organisations for the sake of fighting the bad guys, to the point of exhaustion, one is now spontaneously inclined to participate in humanitarian projects in a free, disinterested and joyful manner. Such transformed masochists will be capable of unfailing endurance, effectiveness and toughness. With this renewed connection to the soul, one finds the joy of creating, participating and contributing. Thus one moves away from calculating service-sacrifice to joyful service, that is both creative and disinterested. This structure is the most conducive to the development of qualities of service and compassion.

Finally, as one is no longer intent on being right in order to justify the pain and all the mechanisms of the structure, one rediscovers good will, one of the most beautiful qualities of the soul. This quality is a blessing for the world. It is apparently so simple, and yet it is one of the most challenging qualities for the ego. It involves a major capacity for letting go of the basic personality mechanisms of powerlessness and dissatisfaction. When one is able to practice good will on a daily basis in one's actions, one's words, and one's interactions with others, the masochist structure is well on its way to being cured.

- **Declaration of transformation**

> I am the source of everything that happens in my life
> and I have all the power within me to create a free and satisfying life now.
> Life is beautiful, I accept people as they are, I am free.

- **Contribution task**

Thanks to its qualities, this structure is a demonstration of service rendered in joy and detachment, an example of strength and courage. It fosters the creation of a world of mutual support, freedom, respect and love for all on this planet.

5-7 The Masochist Structure – Summary

- **Basic fear of the structure:** fear of being taken in, fear of power.

- **Source experiences in the past:** abuse of power, oppression, annihilation, loss of freedom, exploitation, or experience as a perpetrator filled with guilt.

- **Emotional charge:** sense of powerlessness, anger, rage, fear of authority, sense of injustice, resentment, and jealousy.

- **Defence system:** submission-rebellion, blame, "victimitis".

- **Declaration of the defence system:** "I am suffering, and it's all your fault."

- **Needed work:** Let go of the mechanism of victimhood. Stop blaming others. Eliminate criticism and denigration. Reconnect with one's creative power. Practice good will. Celebrate the joy of living that springs from the soul.

- **Declaration of transformation:**

> I am happy. Life is beautiful!

- **Fundamental quality of the soul to be recovered:**

> Joy, good will, a quiet sense of one's own power.

- **Qualities of the structure, once transformed:** compassion, courage, toughness, reliability (trustworthiness), generosity, respect, excellent support, high qualities of service and self-sacrifice. Expression of love through good will, self-sacrifice and service.

- **Contribution task:**

> Bring the force of compassion, mutual support and service into the world.

Bravo all you masochists, life is beautiful!

[1] The laws of "karma" are complex, and we want to avoid falling into the trap of oversimplification. However, some general tendencies are worth noting. In addition, when we say that the soul "chooses" or "generates", we are expressing in very simple terms what is actually a complex energetic phenomenon. Nevertheless, this phenomenon is generated by the evolutionary plan, and the soul contributes to this plan and is in total agreement with it.

[2] The lifetimes involved in such a cycle are not necessarily successive. There may be other lifetimes in between, where the soul chooses to have its instrument experience something else. When the time is right, this aspect is revisited in a given lifetime. This allows the personality to eventually come better prepared to integrate whatever lesson is embedded in the challenge. Human learning is thus built on successive approximations.

[3] Indeed, let us not forget that these experiences can be our own personal experiences, or they can be experiences lodged in the collective unconscious, that we have chosen to work on through resonance. In both cases however, we are totally responsible for the way we deal with such experiences.

[4] Having to breathe prematurely, when the lungs have not had the chance to get used to the oxygen in the air, causes a painful burning sensation. The unconscious records the pain and immediately draws a conclusion: "Breathing hurts; so I will not breathe any more". The instinct for self-preservation will urge breathing nevertheless, but one will tend to breathe as little as possible since, with each breath intake, the initial experience of pain will constantly hold back the natural impulse to breathe deep. This has very damaging consequences, first of all physically, at the level of energy intake and elimination. Energy intake: the physical body maintains its vitality thanks to its etheric counterpart. When we breathe, we take in more than the chemical components of air: we breathe in etheric particles, called *prana*, in the oriental tradition, or *negative ions* in NASA laboratories, which feed the etheric body. Without this constant nurturing, the body weakens and dies. Elimination: breathing accounts for 70% of our functions related to elimination (3% occurs through bowel movements, 7% through urination, 20% through perspiration, and 70% through breathing). Breathing less means energizing less and eliminating less. Our physical body thus begins its journey rather poorly. This restriction of breathing also leads to emotional energy blocks, and fosters stress (when we want to relax, we take a few deep, sustained breaths), as well as mental blocks (breath control is linked to mental mastery). This bad start in life will thus have debilitating consequences at a basic level, added to all the negative psychological decisions regarding powerlessness and fear that kick in at that moment. Let us mention Van Lysebeth's book entitled Pranayama, as an interesting study of complete breathing and its benefits.

[5] Some good books to read as preparation for conscious birth: Frédéric Leboyer, *Birth Without Violence*; Bernard Montaud, *L'accompagnement de la naissance*, éd. Édit'as; Michel Odent, *Bien naître,* éd. du Seuil.

[6] Frédéric Leboyer, op. cit., pages 75, 77.

[7] Bernard Montaud, op.cit.

[8] This, by the way, is a confirmation of the etheric link which exists between mother and child.

chapter 6

The PSYCHOPATH Structure

POWER, INFLUENCE, SEDUCTION, BETRAYAL

"I am special, unique, look at me with admiration and love me forever."

6-1 Stories

Victor works as a surgeon. The eldest of five children, he was always his parents' favourite, especially his mother's. It must be said that he was quite a remarkable little boy: intelligent, even gifted, always the first in his class, original and endearing in his ways. At the age of six or seven, he could already hold his own in conversations with adults. He also had a great talent for music, which, for his parents, was a subject of pride whenever he would sit at the piano during family gatherings. His parents always held him up as an example to his brothers and sisters, who bowed before his many talents. His father, a doctor, hoped that such an exceptional son would follow in his footsteps. And this is indeed what Victor did when he chose a career as a surgeon.

This profession was perfect for him. He was brilliant, very self-assured, warm and at the same time imposing in the eyes of patients. His authority was unquestionable. He felt he was playing an important role. His patients swore by him; most of the secretaries and nurses had a crush on him. At the hospital, everyone admired him at first, then the admiration turned to loathing and jealousy in the presence of such talent and arrogance. Yet he chafed at the rigid regulations of the hospital, and thought of setting up a private clinic under his own name, where he could be king in his own castle and be free to demonstrate the full scope of his genius.

He was married, and his wife enjoyed strutting next to such a well known and admired figure. Yet she knew he cheated on her constantly. Indeed Victor was a womaniser at heart, and actively surrounded himself with a harem of women who treated him as a god. Their admiration and attachment gave Victor a great deal of satisfaction, and there was no need for him to give much in return. All of these women were constantly being duped. He would make promises he rarely kept, and lied to each and every one of them as needed, and this didn't bother him in the least. As far as he was concerned, he was doing them a great honour just to go out with them, even for just a one-night stand. His seductive power was such that many of them fell for him, and were totally sucked in for a while. He would always make sure he dropped them before they left him.

Victor seemed to enjoy an easy, brilliant lifestyle. He made a lot of money, but spent even more on dates, travels abroad, luxury cars and all manner of excess. Yet he felt that stress was eating him up inside. Sometimes he felt so tense that sleep just wouldn't come. In order to relax, he began to take medication and started drinking alcohol, which made him even more arrogant, impatient and full of himself. Then one day, as he was driving his car completely drunk, he had an accident that left him badly handicapped and unable to continue practising as a surgeon. His women fans vanished like a flock of birds. Bankers foreclosed on his debts. He had to stay home with his wife, who made him pay dearly for all the humiliations, the snide remarks and the cheating she had endured. Victor's glory had left him, and he now faced his moment of truth.

◆   ◆   ◆

Marianne, Victor's sister, did not appreciate her brother's achievements. As a result of being constantly exposed to this model of perfection throughout her childhood years, she was riddled with self-doubt, and understood that in order to be loved, if you didn't have any special talents, you had to at least look good. Feeling deeply wounded by a sense of inferiority to her brother, she chose to attract attention and love by being nice. So she became a loveable, refined woman who uses all her assets to gain love and approval. Always smiling, available and ready to listen to other people's cares, she will do anything to please. She lives in constant fear of falling short of perfection, and always makes sure to avoid responsibility, so as not to risk making mistakes. So she just takes on occasional translation contracts, which allow her to pay the bills and buy whatever she needs to look good, without taking any chances. One time, however, as a result of her charm, she was offered an important position in the field of public relations. She accepted, feeling her time had finally come, but she ended up in such a state of tension that she had to quit her job after a few months, disappointed and very angry, as she was unable to simply accept her failure and move on to better things. In her relationships, she tends to unconsciously recreate the relationship she had with her older brother by choosing brilliant men (or seemingly so) who are full of themselves. This keeps feeding her lack of self-confidence, and increasing the need for approval that she carries within herself. The superficial smiles and automatic niceness require more and more energy on her part. Her life seems like a race for recognition and love in ever increasing measures, and she is beginning to run out of steam.

◆   ◆   ◆

Nicole is a Director of public relations in an international manufacturing company dealing in luxury clothing. She is a brilliant, driven woman, who radiates passion and energy wherever she goes. As an only child, she feels she had a happy childhood. Even as a little girl, she was cute and attracted everyone's attention with her charm and her lively spirit. Her father adored her and was very proud of her. Her mother, a rather withdrawn woman, was not a very significant person in her life. Her teenage years, on the other hand, were a difficult period. First of all, her family's material circumstances, which had been very prosperous, took a turn for the worst, and Nicole had to learn to live very simply, even to the point of poverty, which was very unpleasant for her. Then her parents ended up separating, as they had never really got along. Her father went to live with another woman he was very much in love with. He took less and less interest in Nicole, who experienced this event as a major betrayal, leaving a permanent scar in her heart.

But she made up for all this by building a career for herself. She knew how to get her way and move ahead, so that now she has a job that matches her ability. She is in charge of organising all the major presentation events of the company where she works, both in Europe and in North America. She loves dealing with the public. She is an excellent animator and makes sure that everything she organises works out perfectly. It matters to her that the people she meets remember her as a special, exceptional person.

To this end, she works non-stop, day and night. She lives in a constant state of stress to ensure that everything is absolutely perfect. She works herself ragged so as to be sure of getting only compliments. Any imperfection, any complaint one might have about her work would be unbearable. Her performance just has to be impeccable, otherwise she feels devastated. Yet no matter what happens, Nicole is always smiling, and apparently in a great mood. Maintaining this image requires a great deal of energy, and generates a lot of stress, but she can't help trying always to look good. She is very hard on her subordinates, demanding the impossible and making them constantly live in the same state of stress she is in.

Her marriage is not a great success. Her husband, who is more the masochist type, does his best to put up with this exuberant, self-centred woman who expects everyone to cater to her. He is very attached to her, as she is very attractive, yet he suffers in silence. This doesn't really matter, as far as Nicole is concerned, as long as he is there and continues to adore her. In any case, in her line of work, she has many opportunities to meet very interesting men who admire her and shower her with compliments and dazzled looks. She is not really interested in having affairs, since she is far too busy with her performance at work. As long as she gets that admiring attention, that's enough for her.

This goes on for over ten years. Along the way her husband leaves her, and her children, who are now teenagers, are beginning to rock the boat. Indeed she had been very domineering and controlling towards them, demanding, in effect, the same performance standards she set for herself. After ten years of this intense level of performance, Nicole has a burnout that forces her to stop all external activities. This is very hard on her. She ends up alone and distraught, face to face with herself. The moment of truth has finally come for her also.

◆   ◆   ◆

Victor, Marianne and Nicole are all caught in the psychopath structure. This mechanism is based essentially on the need for recognition, approval and love which in turn generates a need for power and influence on as many people as possible in order to maintain this recognition. This is a complex structure which can generate behaviours that are either very primary or quite subtle and refined, depending on the individual concerned. In this context, we will focus on its most direct manifestations. But as the need for love is inherent in human nature, we will find certain aspects of this structure in nearly everyone, in a more or less acute form. We shall begin our attempt to shed light on this structure by examining its sources in past lives and in childhood.

6-2 Past life experiences at the root of the psychopath structure

According to our observations, this type of structure is founded on past lives where the person had a great deal of power and influence, and enjoyed very special status: king, queen, prince or princess, despot, high ranking political figure, high flying call girl, army chief, director of a large commercial or prostitution network, very wealthy person, religious leader, great healer, famous personality for one reason or another, indeed any influential position, often combined with domination and exploitation. The individual was admired and served, most often as a result of manipulation, seduction or fear rather than genuine gratitude and recognition. He could easily abuse his power. The ego, at its low level of evolution, has reclaimed these situations to create a sense of strength, to feed himself, fill himself with conceit and arrogance, and end up believing in his own specialness, his invulnerability, his superiority to others, and his right to boundless love and admiration. This type of situation is ideal for the ego to build a false identity based on the influence and power one has over people.

Another factor is generally present, giving a powerful emotional charge to the structure: betrayal. Indeed, all those people who were despised, seduced or used in some way will naturally end up rebelling, either alone or as a group, and betray this figure whom they had apparently adored and served, or simply bowed to in the past. Thus the situation generated by the psychopath structure is a **position of great power and influence on people followed by the loss of that power through betrayal**. This is a major shock for the ego, as it thought of itself as being almighty, invulnerable, and the object of eternal recognition. At the moment of betrayal, all this false identity caves in like a house of cards.

Maggie is the daughter of a poor craftsman living in Paris at the time of Louis XV. Her childhood is spent in the streets, and she has to start working at a very young age in her father's shop in order to help provide for the needs of the family. Sometimes she sees beautiful carriages go by with finely dressed people inside, and she wonders why she can't live that way herself. This makes her very angry. When she reaches the age of adolescence, her father becomes ill, and the shop is closed. She is sent to work as a chambermaid for a nobleman, in a magnificent residence. An old servant woman goes through the requirements of her new assignment with her. She listens with one ear, all absorbed in marvelling at the luxury all around her. She gets into her rather unrewarding work, that nevertheless gives her an opportunity to be with important people. Maggie dreams of one day sitting at the same table with them. She grows up, becoming more and more beautiful with each passing year. One day a visitor notices her and invites her to his home. He asks for her favours and, in return, promises to provide a much more pleasant lifestyle than that of a servant girl. Maggie doesn't hesitate for a moment: this is her chance. Thus she is introduced into this circle of noble people, and one day catches the eye of a relative of the King himself. Thus she joins the King's Court. Her talent for seduction and her beauty allow her to get just about anything she wants. She lives a glorious lifestyle, becoming more and more arrogant and sure of her own power. After several years enjoying this position of prestige, Maggie begins to lose some of her attractiveness. Not to mention the fact that she has generated a fair amount of animosity among the women around her. Sensing the wind turning, she decides to take part in a plot to discredit a young person she feels is upstaging her, and thus regain her dominant position. Unfortunately, she is betrayed by one of her close friends; the plot is uncovered and fails. Maggie is arrested and thrown in jail, then sent to a convent as a servant girl. There she spends the remainder of her life in the bitterness and anger of wounded pride. The defence system is set up: "In order to hang onto power and its attendant benefits, I need to seduce and manipulate even more, and I must beware of everyone."

We are in the Middle East, sometime around the Tenth Century. Omir, the youngest son of a sultan, used to being served and venerated, reaches adulthood and becomes the spiritual leader of the land. His elder brother helps his father with political matters, since he is the one who will eventually inherit the title. For his part, Omir already reigns like a master on all religious matters. Feeling self important and full of his "connection with God", he uses his power abusively, especially with women, by imposing religious laws that take away all of their freedom. The father, who is deeply religious and sees his son as a new messiah, bows to all his requests. This tyranny lasts for years. Then the sultan dies and is replaced by his eldest son. The latter had never said a word until then, suppressing a growing sense of jealousy towards his brother, who had enjoyed his father's unconditional support as he imposed his will on the people. This jealousy and rancour were shared by many others who had suffered from the religious leader's intransigence. Thus, shortly after gaining access to the throne, the new sultan stripped his brother of all his powers, sending him to prison and having him stand trial for distorting religious teachings. Omir was sentenced to death. After being exposed for several days chained to the gates of the palace so that the population could taunt him and witness his destitution, he was executed.

At that moment, the ego's wounded pride, anger, fear and all the emotional reactions triggered by this situation generated a series of distinct active memories which formed the defence system of the psychopath structure: "If I want to be safe, I need to hang onto power even more doggedly so as never to be betrayed. I have to make sure that *everyone* is *always* on my side."

Often a shameful death, imprisonment or a miserable life may immediately follow this betrayal. The king becomes a slave, for example. The pride-inflated ego is then heavily confronted. The individual ends up leaving this plane of existence with a very powerful emotional charge deeply imprinted in his memories: "If I want to hang onto power along with the sense of identity I got as a result of my influence on people, I should concentrate on this even more and take care never to be betrayed. The worst thing that could happen to me would be to lose other people's recognition. I must avoid this at all cost, it hurts too much." The individual carries this defence system away with him, so as to avoid any future suffering of the kind that he was unable to integrate. He carries it with him, ready for reactivation at the start of a subsequent lifetime.

6-3 Present life experiences which foster the recreation of a psychopath structure

When the Self chooses to work on the personality at the level of this type of memory, the early childhood circumstances chosen for reactivation will essentially have to do with family dynamics. The child is often the favourite of one or both parents. He is his mother's darling, or she is daddy's girl, as this works even better if it involves the parent of the opposite sex, though this is not a prerequisite. The individual is often an only child, the eldest, the youngest, or the most gifted. At the outset, he has to be given special status so that pride can begin to take root.

What happens in this situation? The child is excessively "loved" by one of the two parents, who generally projects an ideal image on the child as a way to compensate for unconscious emotional dissatisfactions. The child is adored, coddled, spoilt, overprotected. He is given the very best of everything, often to the detriment of the parent. He becomes the focal point of the family. He is important (and he knows it). In fact the parent loves the child yet smothers him with his own unconscious mechanisms, often with the best intentions. Yet the child senses these unconscious expectations and will react accordingly.

The child therefore gets a false experience of love at a very early age. This distortion will form the basis of a whole series of specific behaviours. One of the major features of this structure will be how it reclaims the energy of love for selfish personal motives.

In particular he senses that, in order to preserve this privileged position as the favourite, i.e. this position of power, he has to behave in such a way as to please this parent and satisfy his or her expectations. He thus learns the dynamics of seduction at a very young age. If he conforms to what dad, mom, or adults in general expect of him (they are the ones who have all the power at this time, and the unconscious always makes generalisations), he knows that in return he will consolidate his position as the favourite, therefore his position of power. He learns to perform, seduce, manipulate and project a counterfeit image of himself in order to gain approval and love. Being himself is not enough. In fact it is downright dangerous, since he might not be perfect, and therefore runs the risk of disappointing people and of losing their love and affection. This would mean losing the influence he has on others. Thus he learns to behave for the sake of others, instead of for his own sake, in order to gain the assurance of being loved, of being "perfect" and, if possible, of being the best and the most attractive.

This means that the child will end up being out of touch with himself at a very young age. He does not know who he is exactly, and loses self-confidence. At first he knows he is playing games, but as the years go by, he identifies more and more totally with the roles he plays in order to win people over and manipulate them. He is then caught in the mechanism.[1]

This same type of behaviour can be generated by another family dynamic, where the child may not have a special place but is in some form of competition, for one reason or other, with certain brothers or sisters. The latter may hold a position that the child envies. For example, if the eldest is the favourite and the most brilliant, the younger child will observe this dynamic and envy that position, especially if he carries certain power-related karmic memories. He is confronted on a daily basis with the demonstration that, to be loved, one must be special. He will thus take his brother or sister as a model, according to well known principles, since he or she has what he would like to have, and will spend his life trying to prove that he is also the best.

We have also observed psychopath structures developing in a family environment which seems the opposite of what we have just described, where, for example, there is very little love and the individual is stifled (directly or indirectly through verbal or physical abuse). The child is then deeply wounded in his identity. If he carries memories of power, he may add a psychopathic aspect that demands recognition to a masochist structure developing as a result of feeling stifled. In such cases, the arrogance of the psychopath is combined with the anger and aggressiveness of the masochist, and we get a very strong, brilliant, fascinating structure that is also very destructive and ready to pounce whenever the structures are reactivated.

• Betrayal

To complete the reactivation of deep-set memories, the child may need to experience betrayal directly. This is not absolutely necessary, but it reinforces the memory. Circumstances may widely vary. My observations suggest that this simply occurs gradually as the child grows up. He becomes more and more independent and the parent senses that his little darling has changed; he begins to lose interest. This often happens during adolescence: the child begins to look like an adult, and the parent feels ill at ease. Another classic condition arises when another child is born into the family, and the eldest then loses his privileged status as the focus of interest is shifted to another person. This can also happen in cases of divorce, as the parents' separation drags the children into other relationships that can diminish the individual interest the child enjoyed previously. The physical disappearance of the parent can also produce the same result. No matter what the circumstances, they will be interpreted as a form of betrayal and will thus reinforce the inner defence system.

Even if early childhood conditions are not the particular ones we have just described, it is easy to get caught in the dynamic of seeking love and approval, and thus to recreate the structure, albeit in its less acute aspects. Indeed, as is the case with the masochist aspect, the parent-child dynamic can easily conjure up a dominant/dominated dynamic. Rare are the parents who truly listen to a child's every need without creating some degree of affective alienation. Any child has a genuine need for love, acceptance and support from his parents for his inner development. He needs to be recognised for who he is, as he is. The structure will seek conditions appropriate for its development if that parental love and recognition are not granted in a free and generous manner, or are given with unconscious expectations and attachments, for in such cases the child must earn that love and recognition by pleasing his parents, playing a role, submitting or rebelling, in short by being other than himself. For this reason, we find psychopathic character traits, particularly selfishness, the need for love and sensitivity to other people's opinion in just about everyone.

When the individual leaves home, he will reinforce the dynamic he learnt as a child. In the context of day-to-day relationships (couple, children, fellow workers, friends), he will develop other types of performance and seduction, other masks in order to reinforce his image. This is an unending, hopeless quest for a sense of identity.

As for the other structures, the individual's level of evolution will determine how he reacts to present life circumstances, using them either to reinforce the mechanisms or, on the contrary, to manifest the qualities of his soul.

We can develop certain aspects of the psychopath structure without necessarily getting into all its excessive behaviours. In such cases, the structure is less emotionally charged, and it developed simply because we learned that, in order to be loved, we have to behave according to what other people want from us.

6-4 The Psychopath Structure Defence System

✓ **The underlying fear of this structure:** fear of not being loved, fear of losing one's power of influence, fear of losing other people's approval, fear of not being perfect, fear of losing face, fear of betrayal.

✓ **Emotional charge:** pride, arrogance, need to be loved, need to be popular, lack of self-confidence, egocentricity, selfishness.

✓ **Basic defence system:** seduction. manipulation, performance, emphasis on image, quest for influence, perfectionism, falseness.

✓ **Statement of this structure:**

"ME, I am unique, the most handsome, the most interesting person, here is me, take notice, behold, admire and love me forever, and don't you ever betray me."

In this section, we will give a global description of typical dynamics and behaviours. In actual fact, one needs to keep in mind that there are a wide variety of possible nuances, often very subtle. At this stage, a distinction can be made between different types of psychopaths:

• The "great psychopaths"

These are individuals who really are very talented, and have a higher than average inner level of evolution and personality development. They really are special people. Generally, ever since their childhood, they were very precocious, brilliant, and their level of performance was above average. If they are caught in the structure, these talents will fuel their pride and will be reclaimed in order to gain power and influence, to be popular (to be loved and admired), to dominate and possess other people.

• The "minor psychopaths"

These are less gifted individuals who try to make themselves and others believe that they are special and unique in some way, that they are worth more than the average person. Their behaviour is less exuberant (they are not so well endowed), but they are nevertheless caught in a similar dynamic. With little in the way of real talent, they strive first of all to gain love and recognition. The less talented, the more conceited they are as a compensation for their failures. They are always looking for an avenue, in the form of a person or group, as miserable as they may be, that may lead them to a measure of recognition and influence. As young people, they tend to be brothers or sisters of a very gifted child who has indeed "succeeded", and with whom they will inwardly compete for the rest of their lives.

A distinction can also be made between extroverted and introverted psychopaths:

• Extroverted, active psychopaths

They are exuberant and take up a lot of space; you can't miss them. They have a lot of nerve and are not afraid of being seen, of exhibiting themselves and performing to the hilt. They are governed by the need for appearance and love at all cost, and this is where they get their boldness. People who are caught in this structure and who happen to be very gifted will be in this category because they can afford to behave in this manner. The category can also include less gifted individuals.

• Introverted, passive psychopaths

The various forms of fear are more prevalent for these people. The lack of self-esteem is less hidden, and their seductive play is more discreet. They too will do anything to be loved, but their behaviour will lean towards self-denial, and towards real or symbolic prostitution in order to gain a little love or admiration. These are very nice, adorable people, so much so that one cannot help liking them, at least for a while. Less gifted psychopaths, whose ego is not so strong, will often find themselves in this category. Though this structure can be found in both women and men, women will more often tend to be passive psychopaths. This is understandable, since social pressure tends to condition girls for seduction and passivity.

The characteristics we have just described will apply more to some of these types than to others, with many possible nuances. The roots of the structure remain the same however.

Before we get into a description of the behaviours stemming from this structure, we will take a closer look at the inner dynamics generated by this system. This will make it easier to understand the behaviours later on.

Inner consequences of this defence system:

1- Loss of a genuine sense of identity, lack of self-confidence:

The individual has placed so much emphasis on recognition from other people that he ends up identifying with it. He thus loses any real sense of his own identity, which springs from the soul and is completely independent of what other people think or perceive about him.

Here we find the concept of "persona" as defined in the Larousse Dictionary of Psychoanalysis and in Encyclopædia Universalis:

> "*persona*, a concept introduced by Jung who defined it as follows: "A complex array of functions which developed for purposes of adaptation or necessary commodity, but which is not identical to the individual's personality. (…)" Or: "The persona is a compromise between the individual and society in terms of what the individual seems to be". It is therefore a mask that can work in a positive way only if the subject does not identify with it (…)"

> In a very general sense, the persona gives any social subject three options for deception: "appear in such or such a light", "hide behind this or that mask", "develop an image and behaviour that will serve as a protective wall" (dialogue between the self and the unconscious). We put on an appropriate face for every occasion, we play a social role, we distinguish ourselves through some title (doctor, professor, colonel, etc.), all of these effects spring from this psychic function covered by the persona (…) This task of social integration demands a considerable investment or energy from each subject. It requires hiding entire segments of one's inner life, and leaving unexplored nearly all of an individual's potential (…) The subject needs to learn to master structures of adaptation. But this adaptation, which can be more or less successful as the case may be, is not the end all and be all of psychic life, according to Jung. It is only a condition so that, in a second part of one's life, one can journey "towards self discovery."

It is interesting to note that this structure, which often makes people arrogant, conceited, and full of themselves, is based in fact on a lack of self-confidence, on uncertainty with regards to one's own power.

This loss of his sense of identity generates constant insecurity with regard to what the individual really is. It is because this loss of identity is so painful that he has such outrageous behaviours in terms of seduction and manipulation. He desperately tries to recover a sense of who he is through others, as well as the wholesome and genuine sense of power originating from his soul, which he has lost. This is indeed a hopeless quest, for one does not find oneself through performance, or the admiration and "love" of others.

It must be noted that this lack of self-confidence is very different from that of the masochist structure, where the defence system involves submission or rebellion, where one's identity is stifled, but there is no loss of one's sense of identity: masochists suffer yet they are able to sense who they are, even if they have lost confidence in their own power. Psychopaths don't know who they are, and lose themselves in a constant quest for love. They have also lost their true power, but they replace it with the power of ego.

2- Dependence on other people's opinion

This form of dependence is very widespread; to the extent that one might get the impression that such is human nature. It generates a great deal of suffering. Being independent towards other people's opinion is a sign of great inner maturity as well as a guarantee of freedom. What we are referring to here is genuine freedom, which is flexible and open, not the rigid insensitivity found in the next structure we will examine.

3- Inability to accept oneself as one really is, perfectionism

When one is out of touch with oneself, one cannot experience genuine, simple self-love, and it is very difficult to naturally accept oneself with one's qualities and faults. One is full of expectations with regard to oneself, out of fear rather than in a free and creative way. One wants to be "perfect", either directly out of pride, or because one thinks that this is the way to be loved. But what are the standards on which this perfection is based? This creates a great deal of inner tension.

4- Constant anxiety

Worrying about one's identity and one's performance generates a state of anxiety that is often covered up with hyperactivity. Will one be good enough, interesting enough, brilliant enough, perfect enough to be constantly appreciated and loved, and never betrayed? This anxiety is further fuelled by an ever-present fear of betrayal, which leads to a lack of confidence in others, and thus a constant state of stress.

5- Quest for power in order to feel "loved"

In this structure, there is no point in having power if it is at the expense of being hated by everyone (as is the case with the next structure). On the other hand, gaining power for the sake of recognition, admiration and love from all is of primary importance.

Furthermore, one is not content with just being loved: one needs to be the only object of love, to be the favourite. It is a great source of pain to feel that someone else is getting as much love as oneself, or more. Living becomes a kind of permanent competition for energy, as receiving love or approval, in fact, amounts to receiving energy. There is an urge to monopolise this energy. This generates a different kind of jealousy from that of a masochist, who envies others for their (apparent) happiness: a psychopath envies others and is in competition with them (most often unconsciously) for the sake of recovering his status as the favourite. We can easily see how this can distort or even destroy any relationship.

To love and to be loved is simple and natural at the soul level. The psychopath structure turns this natural flow into a traumatic need because an unresolved emotional charge is attached to it. For this reason, when this structure is active, no matter what one does, no matter what one may gain, it will never be enough to feel truly loved, recognised, and reassured. One will never get this gentle, serene, deep sense of BEING that springs from the presence of the soul. One will never have enough, and will remain in a constant state of worry.

These mechanisms, designed to counteract the loss of real identity, will generate behaviours such as we shall now describe.

6-5 Typical Behaviours of the Psychopath Structure

1) General attitude towards life
• **Self-centredness, arrogance, pride: "I am interesting, SPECIAL and UNIQUE."**

From the outside, the profound lack of self-confidence is totally non-apparent in active psychopaths. On the contrary, they usually seem quite self-assured, exhibiting a great deal of self-esteem and love for themselves, combined with a lot of arrogance, an arrogance laced with charm. They talk about themselves constantly, telling about their lives, their experiences, their exploits, so as to let everyone know (or just about) how special they are and how fascinating their lives are. Passive psychopaths tend to be more discreet, yet will still manage to draw attention to themselves. In order to be loved, one must be special.

In fact, the reason for these theatrics designed to prove how good and interesting they are is that, somewhere in their unconscious, they are not sure at all that this is indeed true. The extent of their pride and conceit is proportional to the degree to which they are out of touch with themselves.

In a professional or social gathering, extroverted psychopaths will never go unnoticed. People just have to see them and take notice. Introverted psychopaths are happy just to quietly radiate, to seduce and to attract attention with their relatively discreet charm.

Let us note that self-centredness may be appropriate for people who are at a low level of development, in order to strengthen ego definition. Indeed, the ego must be well formed so that the soul has a solid instrument at its disposal. Self-centredness can therefore be useful for a while. This is why certain personal development courses focus on "self affirmation". But for people who are more advanced, and who are at the stage of working on liberating egos that no longer need strengthening, the work required involves practising humility, self-effacement and impersonality. The psychopath structure can become a major trap which holds an individual prisoner to the ego and impedes evolution.

• Manipulation, domination: "Adore me!"

If a psychopath finds himself in a position of power, he will abuse it in order to shore up his popularity and to be worshiped by everyone. His ego then feeds on all the energy he gets from other people, which can become like a drug. Losing this popularity is a disaster, for the ego feels as if it is dying.

• Seduction: "Love me!"

In a situation where a psychopath is not in a position of absolute power, he will behave in a very pleasant, charming, seductive, joyful, dynamic, absolutely marvellous way. Psychopaths are very endearing…for a while. After a first encounter with them, people are always totally delighted to have met them. They are consummate practitioners of the art of seduction, which they use in every aspect of their existence.

• Inability to acknowledge mistakes: "I am perfect"

The psychopath's defence system requires the individual to be perfect and to constantly demonstrate this in order to survive. In this structure, it will therefore be impossible to acknowledge one's mistakes. For the unconscious, this is tantamount to dying. So one cannot tolerate any form of criticism, even if it is constructive. Finding fault with the behaviour of a psychopath is to expose oneself to sometimes very violent emotional reactions: he is perfect and he is always right.

• Performance, competition: "I am the best"

Psychopaths are in a constant state of **performance** in order to prove their superiority or maintain their preferred status.

Since they have to be the best, they have to be better than others. This leads them to being in constant **competition** with others. This mechanism can have some good aspects, as it motivates them to surpass themselves in certain areas. They will practice more, study more, think more, etc., which can energise a person in a way. One is "motivated". But this motivation, which stems from an ego desire, generates a great deal of stress. The ego has a limited store of energy and, in such cases, one generally ends up burning out because one is not tapping any real source of energy. In the case of talented individuals, they will become even more entangled in the trap created by their need for recognition, and by the momentary pleasure the ego derives from it. Less gifted individuals will strut their stuff and try to have others believe that they are indeed talented. But sooner or later, they meet someone who is "better" or who is the "favourite". Then comes the pain of recognising that fact, unless they totally deny what is happening and repress this deep into their unconscious. Thus, when one is caught in this structure, one spends hours in stress and anxiety, as one is always, consciously or unconsciously, in a competitive situation. One can only see two types of people: competitors and fans.

- **Appearance matters more than being: "I am my image, which means everything to me, so don't touch it."**

Psychopaths live for the image that seems to define who they are. They create this image on the basis of what they believe they should project in order to gain other people's love and approval, i.e. to feed on their energy. The ego is hung up on appearance, since the experience of "being" is impossible at this level. The psychopath structure nurtures and strengthens this dynamic: "I don't love myself, but the image I have of myself".

One will seek roles that seem important, playing the saviour, the scientist, the healer, the noble soul, the higher being in one form or other. Next to a psychopath, people feel small in relation to such greatness. Yet someone who is truly great at the soul level will elevate another and make him feel great also, as he helps the other person to tune into the richness of his own soul.

In the context of close relationships, psychopaths will often play the saviour-despot, the companion the other cannot do without. What better for one's image than to play the role of a compassionate and loving saviour. This dynamic keeps people in a state of falsehood and alienation which, little by little, destroys the joy of living and generates more and more discontent.

George was the head costume designer in a well known theatre group. He loved his work, where he could create whatever he fancied and be totally original. The director trusted him and gave him a lot of responsibilities. His costumes were indeed very beautiful, showing a lot of creativity. Yet he had problems with some members of the team he managed. Being somewhat full of himself and convinced of his own talent, he demanded perfection and suffered no criticism. As he was caught in a psychopath structure, his authoritarian, conceited attitude rubbed many people the wrong way. His efforts to maintain his image were beginning to take their toll on him when he met Annette, a pretty woman who had just been dumped by her husband. She had accepted a job as prop person for the group, but her frail state of health made it difficult for her to keep up. George took Annette under his wing. He often talked to her, and she found him quite an extraordinary person. Such was her admiration that they ended up getting romantically involved and

decided to live together. Annette was caught in a masochist structure. Though she was
very happy in her relationship with George (she had found her saviour), she felt more
and more sad and ill and couldn't understand why. George spent more and more time
with her, neglecting his work which he was beginning to find too demanding. Indeed a
young assistant had been assigned to work with him, and the latter was becoming more
brilliant than him, which he found difficult to stomach. He was no longer the star.
Though no one questioned his talent, he felt more and more worried. He took himself so
seriously in his saviour role with Annette that it seemed suddenly more important than
his work. (Whenever he was around her and her family, he was still a star.) Thus he
decided to put an end to his artistic endeavours and to take a rather important manage-
rial position in an ordinary company. This office job gave him the opportunity to be more
available to take care of Annette, a victim who had always had a tough life, who was so
much in need of help, and who recognised his greatness.

The illusion was at its peak. Annette was happy, as George was going to be more avail-
able for her. In fact, her victim's structure had just scored a major point ("If I don't have
any power, no one else will either"). George lost a trade that suited him well, but
Annette's family encouraged him in this change. After a few months in his new job,
George realised that he had created a prison for himself. His bosses were demanding, and
no one was swooning before his talents. But it was too late: he had to work in order to
provide for the couple's survival needs. He became more and more stressed, tired, unhap-
py. Meanwhile Annette was not getting any better. It so happened that George also had
a fairly active masochist structure. In fact, this is what had allowed the saviour dynam-
ic to become so overwhelming. The couple sank into gradually increasing depression
and sadness.

When an individual is caught in this structure, he will do anything to preserve
a role or an image that flatters or reassures his ego. As is the case with other structures, he really does suffer, but in this instance, he does not admit it either to himself or to others. Indeed this would mean losing face and having his image tarnished, unless he could create a grand melodrama with his suffering and get a
great deal of public attention. So even if things are not going well, he generally
smiles a broad smile and says that things couldn't be better. He just has to maintain that brilliant image (as opposed to the masochist, for whom nothing is going
right). Only when the physical body breaks down under the self-imposed stress
of maintaining that image for so many years will a psychopath meet his moment
of truth.

• Emotionalism: "I am such a sensitive person."

This structure makes people extremely sensitive emotionally. One is prone to
reacting to just about anything, especially whatever can be interpreted as judgement or criticism. One can throw outrageous fits or sink into deep depression and
sadness (if one's image has been tarnished or if one thinks one is unloved), or fly
to delirious heights of enthusiasm (if one's image has just been spruced up or if
one feels loved). Thus one appears to be a very "sensitive" person. In fact, this
is not the true sensitivity of the soul, but **hypersensitivity of the ego** which is

activated through the memories. Even if the structure is not always that exuberant, we know how most people react very emotionally to other people's opinion.

• Lack of integrity: "I will do anything to be loved and to be admired."

Manipulation, lies, lack of integrity, falsehood, dubious compromises, hypocrisy and game playing are familiar tools. Authenticity, sincerity, frankness, righteousness and loyalty are very scary.

In its introverted aspect, the psychopath structure will not necessarily lead to lying; it takes nerve to lie directly. In this category, fear is the driving force. Yet one will not be totally truthful either. One dodges the issue, pretending to agree, not saying what one really thinks: one acts and lives in falsehood, for the sake of others, for the sake of being loved.

This structure, especially in its extroverted aspect, is characterised by the absence of guilt, yet not in any wholesome way. One seeks other people's approval, yet at the same time one despises and manipulates them unscrupulously, consciously or unconsciously. One is convinced of being right and of being perfect. Guilt will only appear if there is a masochist aspect in the personality; this mechanism is totally alien to the psychopath aspect.

What all of this means is that it is no easy task to disentangle oneself from this structure: as this structure is the most image conscious of all, the process requires a profound re-evaluation of everything one thinks one is. It requires dropping all masks, daring to experience the pain of identity loss, recognising that one has led a false life, daring to confront the truth about oneself, and daring to come to terms with oneself and to love oneself.

2) Relationships: seduction, manipulation, domination, quest for power and influence

SELFISH HEART

Relationships are the number one area where the psychopath structure is likely to be activated. This is where this dynamic really cooks.

When one is caught in this structure, one "loves" only those who love us in return. This conditions all relationships one may have with others, if indeed the word relationship is applicable in this case, since the only person that truly matters is oneself.

• Reclaiming the energy of the heart for selfish purposes, seduction: "I pretend to love you so that you love me."

It is easy to be taken in by the power of seduction of this structure, since using the energy of the heart creates a magnetic, very attractive personality. The individual exudes warmth, seems radiant, welcoming, generous, loving and full of vitality. In fact, the energy of the heart is very active, yet completely reclaimed by the ego. It projects this energy all around, and other people respond very favourably, under the mistaken belief that they are loved (they too are caught in the same dynamic).

The extroverted great psychopaths are "charismatic" people who are capable of using emotions to influence and manipulate even large crowds. When we observe the characteristics of the great crowd movers throughout history, we often find that they share characteristic psychopathic traits. The life histories of television and movie celebrities are also very good examples of this structure. Minor psychopaths are usually small-time charmers doing their thing simply with the people closest to them.

• Inability to love

The psychopathic personality aspect leads to a disconnectedness from the true source of love. To love is to turn one's attention to someone else, but this structure is essentially focused on itself, despite what appear to be the best intentions. For such individuals, other people exist only as instruments to validate their own existence. This is carefully hidden (from others as well as oneself) behind the image of an open, loving and generous person.

This structure makes it impossible to experience a genuine healthy couple relationship, as the energy of love emanating from the soul is short-circuited by the ego. This is perhaps the most limiting structure in terms of genuine, true expression of love. In the case of individuals who are more advanced on the spiritual path, this dynamic often leads to a very painful split between the will of the soul, which is truly inclined to love, and the will of the ego, that wants to please, to possess and to dominate. This is a difficult stage to go through.

• Dominant vs. dominated

Consciously or unconsciously, psychopaths nurture a sense of dependency. In the context of a couple relationship, they will generally choose a partner with a structure that can easily be dominated or manipulated (schizo, oral or masochist). A male psychopath, being a ladies' man, will tend to choose passive-type women, who will admire this tall, handsome man, so strong, so brilliant, so loveable. He will strive to match the mythical image of the powerful, glorious male, the protector of the weaker sex, a most prevalent myth in the collective unconscious (we need only go to the movies to be swamped with such images). He is just not interested in an independent, self-reliant woman who might be more intelligent than him. He would instantly start competing with her.

A female psychopath will be a very attractive, irresistible seductress, using her femininity, her beauty and her sexuality to manipulate, dominate and make people love her. She may perhaps be less obviously arrogant, more subtly brilliant. If she is content with just one partner, he will have to be an unconditional admirer.

Psychopaths will always choose partners who, in some way or other, seem less advanced or less talented than they are. They can thus feel larger and stronger than life. What is important to them is to secure their attachment so as to be sure of being loved and never betrayed. This generates the prime model of an alienating relationship involving a dominant/dominated dynamic.

The couple will endure to the extent that the psychopath can dominate and feel that the other remains an unconditional admirer. Once the initial honeymoon stage is over, it is easy to imagine the endless problems that can arise, always leading to disappointment and heartache. Depending on the structures involved, a dominant/dominated couple can last a long time, or it will explode, often in dramatic and spectacular ways.

• The need for a large audience

Psychopaths are born charmers, and they just cannot help trying to win people over. Yet one person's admiration is simply not enough. They need recognition from everyone: spouse, lovers, mistresses, and also parents, friends, colleagues at work. They need an audience.

• Infidelity, lack of integrity

In the context of a couple relationship, an individual caught in this structure will generally not be satisfied with just one partner-admirer; so he is generally unfaithful, inclined to have many "affairs" (except in cases where the structure is combined with other structures that counterbalance this tendency). His "official" partner will never give him enough admiration and love for him to be satisfied. He will stay in the relationship as long as the other continues to love him despite his escapades. His infidelity will not make him feel the least bit guilty and, to keep the lines open with his numerous conquests, he will not hesitate to lie and to cheat without batting an eyelash.

If he is faithful, he will demand exclusive and unconditional love from his partner. He uses exclusiveness to reassure himself and satisfy his need to be the favourite. In such cases he will be very possessive and domineering, both towards the spouse and towards the children. It is easy to imagine all the emotional reactions of fear, envy and expectation that are all the more powerful since emotions tend to run skin deep in this structure.

• Looking or competing for admiration

In the context of personal relationships, as in other areas of activity, psychopaths cannot see anything but admirers and competitors in the people around them. They tend to surround themselves with people of the opposite sex. Indeed, they will make maximum use of their power of seduction over the opposite sex. So it is easy for them to maintain a court of admirers.

On the other hand, they always feel immediately competitive with people of the same sex. Male psychopaths cannot stand men who can potentially upstage them, and female psychopaths see other women primarily as rivals.

The powerful emotional charge projected by psychopaths easily generates emotional reactions in others. While they may be worshiped by their admirers, they can just as easily be judged very harshly by the people around them (especially by other psychopaths). In particular, they generate a lot of envy. People are never neutral and calm around them: one either loves them or hates them.

• Betrayal

Following the initial honeymoon stage, where they have fallen under the spell of a psychopath, people will end up realising what is actually going on in terms of dynamics, or will simply be reactivated by his behaviour. For this reason, revulsion and loathing will often end up replacing the love and admiration he strove so hard to generate. Indeed his seductive attitude makes him look like he is always promising something; then people end up waiting, in a state of expectation, and nothing ever comes of it. One way or another, the people around him find themselves being reactivated in their own structures, and tiring of his antics, refusing to continue playing the game and eventually turning away from him: the betrayal scenario is then recreated. Even if the individual is not attached to the person who has just dumped him in this manner, this will be a very painful experience, as it will reactivate the primary experience of betrayal. Thus he keeps recreating the conditions at the source of his defence system, and constantly reinforcing them with his behaviour.

3) Sexuality

True to form, a psychopath will use sexual activity as a way of performing and winning people over.

4) The physical body
• Body shape

Due to their highly developed heart energy and their psychological attitude of self-importance, psychopaths share the common physical feature of a wide, outwardly projecting chest, carrying the word ME in large virtual letters. The physical body is generally well proportioned, especially since the psychopath structure and the rigid structure (which we will examine further on) often overlap (rigid people also have an attractive physical appearance).

The eyes are insistent, magnetic, as eye contact is used as a tool to influence people. It is very easy to be taken in by the "warm" expression in a psychopath's eyes. And he is always smiling, since this is an effective tool for manipulation in an emotional society where nearly everyone is seeking to feel loved.

• Health

As far as health is concerned, psychopaths will never admit to being sick, since this is not good for their image and makes them vulnerable, unless it happens to be a spectacular illness with the potential to become a major topic of conversation and to make them special. In such cases, the illness is used to attract attention. If a psychopath manages to heal himself through some cure or discipline, it is a safe bet that we will hear about it at great length. It will be the miracle of the century. Otherwise, he says he is always doing marvellously well and, in the next breath, starts telling you about his latest exploits so that you know how extraordinary life is, and of course, by the same token, how extraordinary he is.

Having for years repressed a basic anxiety, psychopaths end up paying the price in their body. As physical ailments have been denied for a long time, they are generally subject to accidents or serious illnesses that strike them all at once: burnout, heart attacks, cancer. Meanwhile, they will do whatever they can to cover up their stress and unease. They will readily turn to alcohol and hard drugs, as well as a whole spectrum of stimulating medications, so as to always feel in top shape for the sake of their performance and appearance. Unless they are already involved in a consciousness expanding process, they will have no respect for their body, and subject it to excessive stimulation, as the structure demands a constantly high level of energy. At one point, the body can no longer withstand this constant overload, and breakdowns occur. For this structure, illness can then be an opportunity for major awakening.

After years of intensive training, Bertrand is selected to take part in the Olympic swimming competitions. He ends up among the top athletes, then goes on to hold two world records. He becomes an honoured guest everywhere: a star athlete showered with honours, women, money… the world is at his feet. This goes on until one day, during a road trip, the rear axle of the truck just ahead of him comes off and smashes into his car. For Bertrand, this will mean hospitalisation for a year, and seven operations, particularly in the pelvis, knees and ankles. He is then abandoned by all, and utterly alone: an intense time of introspection that will change the course of his life, turning it towards generous service through training young swimmers.

• Automatic choices in clothing

In this structure, physical appearance, like everything else, is used not only to win people over but also to attract attention. Psychopaths place a great deal of emphasis on clothes and outward appearance, in order to reinforce the image they want to project: so they will choose clothes that are original, flashy, special, unique. They just cannot go unnoticed.

5) The energy aspect

A lot of energy is concentrated at the level of the chest and head; on the other hand, there is little energy in the legs and lower part of the body. Individuals who are caught in this structure are always very emotional, and not very grounded.

Psychopaths always exude a great deal of energy, which constantly erupts in flamboyant talk and performance. Their energy is intrusive, bubbly, stimulating, but it soon becomes draining. Their spectacular antics (overflowing "love", excessive service, overwhelming good humour) are sure to draw everyone's attention. They do this not for the sake of stuffing, as in the case with the oral structure, but rather for the sake of dominating and generating attachment in other people. Their brand of energy "pumping" is much more elegant, and better hidden behind radiant appearances, than in the case of the oral structure. Nevertheless, psychopaths are constantly in need of emotional food. They pump energy from all those who enter their circle or relationships.

6) Relating to the material world and money

In this structure, there is no special attention directed towards material things, except when they enhance one's image. One may be interested in acquiring possessions and wealth to the extent that these confer power and allow the individual to stand out among others. In such cases, pride and conceit over one's possessions are to be expected. Psychopaths will not keep money stashed in the bank, as the oral or rigid structures might do. They will externalise their affluence in the form of luxury homes, secondary residences, yachts, race horses, private planes, etc. Less wealthy individuals will nevertheless spend primarily on image enhancing objects. Whatever the situation may be, they will generally live above their means, unless the structure is combined with an active rigid structure.

Some psychopaths, on the other hand, are prepared to sacrifice material security for the sake of fame, popularity or glory (public or private). In such cases, there is no attachment towards material possessions as such, but rather an attachment to the power and influence that they confer in today's society. Some will even glorify themselves as being uninterested in money, as being involved in selfless service. For people with this structure, as long as they find something that allows them to project a flashy image and to attract other people's admiration, the material aspect can be of relatively little importance.

7) Relating to power

Throughout the preceding paragraphs, we have seen this structure's dynamic with regard to power: it is the basic traumatic dynamic common to psychopaths, the one that underscores all of their behaviours. Obviously this "power" gained through manipulation and seduction is nothing but false power, which crumbles sooner or later since it does not rest on any genuine inner strength. Those who are seduced or impressed expect something in return, which never comes, until they eventually arise out of their stupor: that is when the psychopath's influence evaporates and "betrayal" emerges, i.e. the loss of that false power.

• How minor psychopaths and great psychopaths relate to power

It is delicate to describe the psychopath structure. It is difficult to give an average description in terms of its characteristic behaviours. Indeed, this dynamic applies to a wide spectrum of levels of evolution. "Minor psychopaths" are primarily looking for an identity through this structure. Their power is limited, and their circle of influence is relatively small. It usually centres around family members, a few friends, a few working relationships, a few lovers or mistresses if need be.

On the other hand, when this structure affects people at a higher level of development, people who have had time to develop a very rich personality, their circle of influence can expand to a much broader, or even global scale. Great psychopaths primarily play at the highest level of power.

For this reason, this structure is often chosen by highly evolved people. These old souls, as they are often referred to, have had time to develop a lot of genuine qualities: uncommon artistic talents, superior scientific knowledge and intellectual development, impressive esoteric knowledge or psychic powers, etc. All of this baggage places these individuals beyond the current norm, on the personality level, and this gives them far more power than ordinary people. They can make a great difference, positively or negatively. What will they do with this power? Will they make it serve their fellow human beings, or will they use it to feed their structure, as elegant and refined as it may be? This is the challenge for this structure.

8) Work

As we saw earlier on, an individual with this structure will tend to choose a line of work where he is in contact with a lot of people and has plenty of opportunities for role-playing. He will often end up in positions of power where he can gain popularity and influence, and eventually demonstrate his superiority. On the other hand, he will always want a certain level of freedom of movement in order to practice his originality and influence as he sees fit. This structure will be found both in well established professions and in marginal environments, as long as there is an audience: politicians, lawyers, doctors, professors and teachers of all kinds, performance artists, theatre directors, therapists, spiritual leaders, healers, gurus, etc. A job in sales can also be appropriate in our society where, unfortunately, sales are often associated with manipulation. Let us note, once again, that these jobs are not the issue. All we are saying is that the psychopath structure can more easily play out its mechanisms in these types of occupations.

9) Service

The concept of self-denial and impersonal service is obviously foreign to the reality of this structure.

10) Pitfalls in spiritual seeking

Psychopaths will not engage in a process of inner work, or any real self questioning, or digging deep within themselves, as this is the worst thing for them. It generally takes a major physical or psychological ordeal for them to be jolted into awareness. Yet, as is the case with other structures, they may be impelled by their soul to become interested in a process of personal growth. But built-in resistance at the personality level can quickly reclaim this process unless the individual is very vigilant.

When a psychopath is on a spiritual quest, he generally does not remain a student for very long. He soon begins to compete with whoever is teaching him, and quickly promotes himself as master and teacher in his own right. He then surrounds himself with people who are looking for some sort of authority and who are willing to admire him for his great wisdom and knowledge.

Spiritual advancement confers power and influence. This is why some people get caught in the dynamics of this structure, though they may have a great store of spiritual knowledge. Though they may be spiritually advanced, that does not mean that they are necessarily free from the clutches of their egos, especially where pride is concerned.

While we are on this subject, evolution is not a linear process. One might think that the more the soul is present in a personality, the more the personality will tend towards perfect harmony. The reality here is somewhat more complex. The light of the soul in a personality is like the sun shining over a garden: if the garden is well tended by the gardener, the sun will cause many beautiful things to grow. But if the garden is overgrown with weeds, the sun will stimulate the latter as well, which will become more and more pervasive to the point of stifling all that was good. This is why we see some brilliant, intelligent people fall prey to the temptations of the personality despite a high level of awareness. The last and greatest pitfall on the spiritual path, the ultimate test for the ego before being ready to receive more light from the soul, is the test of power. This is why the soul may choose to have an advanced personality experience this structure, in order to test its ability to use power in an impersonal, altruistic manner.

11) Some practical suggestions and tasks leading to transformation

This structure, like all the others, is a vehicle for evolution towards higher levels of awareness, and it must be understood from this perspective. It carries tremendous potential within it. Striving towards an ideal can be a very positive thing. But one must learn to differentiate between true values, values that stem from higher consciousness, and could be likened to "models" that help an individual to become free, and the coercive ideals that this structure tends to generate. Yet even these ideals are stepping-stones on the way to discovering one's true nature. This is the focus of its transformation.

> When masks fall one after another, when psycho-cultural models run out of steam, here I am at this important meeting with myself, with my fundamental identity base (Self). Being aware of who I am and who I aspire to be as an affirmative power, I can thus fully manifest my truth in total awareness of my true essence.[2]

Working on this structure is not easy, and it requires a great deal of finesse. An individual caught in this structure has been wounded in his very essence, and the scar runs deep. For this reason, despite the excessive attitudes resulting from this dynamic, one must not forget the soul searching for itself behind these images and trying to recover its freedom. A psychopathic personality needs to reconnect with the true meaning of love. We can extend our compassion to these individuals as the best form of support that can help them on their own way towards their inner light.

On a personal level, in order to loosen the grip of this structure and allow its better qualities to emerge, one will have to find a way back to simple, genuine self-love and love for others. To this end, one will work on the following aspects:

—let go of the exaggerated sense of self importance that comes with this structure, develop a sense of impersonality;

—learn simple self-acceptance and self-love, take oneself as one is, including faults and qualities;

—stop trying to be perfect; learn from one's mistakes;

—stop being afraid of other people's judgements;

—stop trying to seduce, perform, role-play; stop being afraid to be real, simple, humble, sincere and natural;

—respect others and learn to love them unconditionally;

—learn to give power to others, freely and joyfully;

—free oneself from the deep anxiety stemming from the fear of betrayal.

On a day-to-day basis, one will strive to cultivate simplicity in concrete ways (in all aspects, whether practical or psychological), as well as humility and integrity. Learning to always be rigorously honest with oneself and with others is the most effective discipline for this structure. The most direct way to work on this structure is to be particularly attentive to truth and authenticity, especially in relationships.

For the extroverted aspect of this structure, anything that fosters inner focus is recommended:

—solitude, meditation, silence, genuine listening to oneself and to others;

—practising self-sacrifice and self-denial on a daily basis;

—taking part in unspectacular service activities where there is no chance of attracting attention. Service rendered discreetly enlightens the soul;

—one can also practice "ego fasts", i.e. spend a whole day without ever saying the word "me" and without talking about oneself;

—take less interest in one's external appearance (for example, a woman may dare to go out without make-up);

—compliment other people, and focus attention on them.

For the introverted aspect, anything that fosters genuine self-expression is beneficial. Theatre, in particular, which is not recommended for extroverted psychopaths, can be a fine opportunity to dare to manifest oneself, to risk making mistakes and losing face in front of an audience. Surviving such an experience and integrating it can be very useful for this structure.

6-6 The Psychopath Structure Transformed

Transformed psychopaths have a wealth of wonderful qualities, which are often the opposite of their ego characteristics, as is the case with other structures:

One of the first qualities to emerge will be a **great capacity for impersonal love and service**. Everything that was used for seduction purposes is now used for the sake of love and service. A doctor will treat his patients with care and generosity; a teacher will be available to his students, forgetting his own needs so that his students may succeed (even better than himself); a politician will listen to those who elected him and trust him, and will do his best to serve them; an artist will perform for the love of his art, of his audience, out of his own genuine inspiration; a mother will raise her children with respect for their freedom and need for self-reliance, offering support without imposing her influence, etc. As soon as healing and transformation take place, **all the richness of love becomes available**. The individual is able to invest all of his talents in effective, original, selfless and generous service activities. Through joyful and impersonal contribution, offered in a selfless manner, the individual can manifest all of his qualities for the greater good of all.

A transformed psychopath will always be **brilliant and interesting**, but in a pleasant, nurturing way for the people around him, for he now knows how to use his qualities to confer energy on others, to radiate this energy genuinely and simply. He gives without attachment. The false pretence at radiating love is transformed into real presence and into genuine human warmth.

He becomes a **joyful player**; full of true joy, since the stress is no longer there, and neither are the counterfeit smiles.

He will still have this aspect of **creative originality**, for he is not afraid of breaking new ground, but he will create according to the truth within himself. This will make him a tremendously deep and pleasant person to be with. As he still has this "special", original aspect, people will continue to notice him, of course, but he will not emphasise this for purposes of ego inflation. He will simply be happy to be able to contribute in some way.

Being a master in the art of influence, he will use this strength to **inspire others** to reconnect with their soul, to extend themselves and find their true source of power. With all these lifetimes of training in the art of listening to others and understanding them in order to better manipulate them, he will now use this strength, this finesse and insight, to better understand people and support them with profound respect for who they are. He will be an **excellent teacher**, in any field, supporting his students on the way to discovering and expressing their full potential. His **intuitive knowledge of human nature** allows him to excel in all occupations involving interpersonal relationships.

With his originality, the individual will live in **total integrity**, not caring about what other people might think. He will excel in the art of negotiation and diplomacy, and will be able to exert influence with integrity.

His charisma and qualities of verbal expression, which are often highly developed, will be used to **inspire people**. Thus he will be an excellent spokesperson for humanitarian causes which he will defend with gusto, but also with integrity and without any personal agenda. He can also be an excellent counsellor. The heart energy becomes available once again to create, to love and to serve.

In short, all the qualities, all the knowledge which the individual had developed in order to satisfy his ego, are now invested in serving others, serving the cause of freedom and truth, serving his own soul.

• Declaration of transformation

> "I love, unconditionally and freely.
> I am truthful with myself and with others.
> I use my power to love and to serve."

• Contribution task

To set an example of power serving the purposes of love

What a program! This structure will generate exceptional capacities for contribution. In fact, everyone experiences this type of structure sooner or later, and then transforms it, as it is the structure with the strongest link to power. Once transformed, it will simply manifest the power of the soul in the world. All of the talents, wealth, knowledge, and powers that the individual has developed are now dedicated to serving humanity.

His greatest contribution is to be
an example of liberation from the power of the ego,
and the manifestation of the power of the soul
through genuine love, impersonality and self-sacrifice.

1 In some respects, this ties in with the development of the "ideal self" as defined by Freud. According to the Larousse Dictionary of Psychoanalysis: "An expression which describes, in Freudian terms, an entity or a differentiated form of the self that springs from narcissism (the young child is his own ideal model) and from the parental model which acts as the child's reference point, both as a prohibitive principle and as an ideal for self-identification... Each individual, writes Freud, is part of several groups, he is bound through identification to several sides, and has developed his ideal self on the basis of a wide variety of models."

6-7 The Psychopath Structure – Summary

- **The underlying fear of the structure:** fear of not being loved, of losing one's power and influence, fear of betrayal.

- **Source experiences in the past:** position of power followed by betrayal, trauma related to the loss of power.

- **Emotional charge:** pride, arrogance, selfishness, need to be loved, need for popularity.

- **Defence system:** seduction, manipulation, performance, importance of cultivating one's image, quest for influence and power, falsehood.

- **Declaration of the defence system:** "Love me."

- **Work to be done:** let go of the need to be loved, recover one's true identity, reconnect with the source of genuine love.

- **Declaration of transformation:**

> I use my power to love and to serve.

- **Fundamental qualities of the soul to be recovered:**

> Real love, impersonality, humility, simplicity, self-sacrifice.

- **Qualities of the structure, once transformed:** genuine LOVE, human warmth, compassion, generosity, originality, creativity, high energy, integrity, humour, intelligence, inner wealth.

- **Contribution task:**

> Set an example of power serving the cause of love in all areas of human activity.

Bravo all you Psychopaths, we love you just the way you are !

The RIGID Structure
EMOTIONAL SHUT-DOWN
"The insensitive one"

7-1 Stories

John is a bank manager. He is married, with four children, with whom he is very strict. He lives in a very nice, extremely well kept house, in the suburbs west of the city. He started working at this job as soon as he graduated from university, and has not changed since, getting regular promotions due to his dedication to his work. He owns two cars, one for himself and one for his wife, which he trades in every two years. Yet he is always faithful to the same brand, simply upgrading to the latest models. His life is carefully planned, and there is not much room for the unexpected, which he can't stand in any case.

He makes it his duty to have regular family visits, which he plans several months in advance. These visits are generally very chilly, since John does not feel any warm ties with his parents, any more than with his brothers and sisters. His father, a notary, has never shown any signs of affection (this is just not done among men), and his mother, a small self-effacing woman who has spent her life serving everyone, carries on as usual with near total discretion and silence. During these visits, they talk about this and that, about material projects (buying a new secondary home, a new car, a new type of lawnmower), or sometimes about politics, but in a neutral way, without any intensity. As for holidays, these are also planned at least a year in advance, with everything paid in full at the time when reservations are made. As for sports, John regularly plays tennis once a week, and he set up a special exercise room in his house, with several body building machines, in order to stay in shape. Every morning, he spends twenty minutes working out, and nothing could make him break this routine. John is always very well dressed, in conservative, elegant clothes. He is a "handsome" man who always looks good.

With his children, he maintains this same rigid rule by constantly monitoring their homework and their socialising. His wife is also subject to the same conditions, and there is no talking back. He can't stand pets, and has always refused to have any at home, despite repeated pleas from his children. The only times he has been known to come out of his cool impassiveness, to the point of angry outbursts, was when there was talk of having a dog in the house. It was as if someone had cut him to the quick. At that time, everyone had bowed to his paternal authority. Once, however, his youngest daughter, Marielle, had come home with a young injured cat she had found on the street. Out of duty, he had agreed to take the animal to the veterinarian. The cat was looked after, and quickly regained its vitality. It ran everywhere around the house, and even dared to pounce on John as he was reading the Financial Post. This was too much for John, and the next morning, when he noticed that the cat had peed on the kitchen floor because the door to the basement, where the litter box was kept, had been closed by mistake, he said that the time had come to get rid of the animal. Marielle had a fit and began to cry when she heard this, promising her dad that she would take even better care of the cat from now on, and that it would never again make such a mess and that it would always be quiet. The cat was not impressed by the paternal verdict, and continued to bring joy and a touch of craziness into the household. John became more and more impatient, and one day the cat disappeared. Marielle looked for it for several days, in tears and grief at having lost her dear little friend, until her dad told her that he had taken this little devil to the SPCA so that others might take care of it. His daughter's tearful pleading to take the animal back was to no avail, and he remained inflexible. There would be no more animals in the house, and that was that.

John was never sick. He was very proud of his job and of his family. His life was a "success", and everything was under control. He was very pleased and satisfied with this state of affairs, and he wondered why people had so many problems. Life was not so complicated, after all, if one would only take the trouble to organise it properly.

John had a regular cash flow, and he began to get seriously involved in stock investments. Everything was going well. After some fifteen years of this perfectly organised and well planned life, things began to change. The children were now adolescents, and the house became the scene of frequent disputes. John could not understand what was going on. He was losing control over his children. His eldest son had taken his car one evening, without permission, and had brought it back with a big dent in the side (a three month-old car!). He gave his son a stern lecture on principles, as the son listened without a word. Some time later, his youngest son was brought home by the police because he was caught under the influence of drugs. John was horrified. He hoped that the neighbours had not seen any of this: what an embarrassment! He now had to lecture his youngest son as well. This kind of situation became more and more frequent. His daughter wanted to quit school and go hitchhiking in India with her boyfriend! Really, now, what was this wind of insanity that was suddenly rocking his family? This had to be his wife's fault for not having brought enough discipline into her children's upbringing. In fact she was also behaving in increasingly strange ways. She who had been so perfectly submissive and pleasant was now becoming more and more difficult. She began to argue against his decisions, and even refuse to take part in certain activities, like going with him to an evening of bridge at the General Manager's home, for instance, saying these evenings bored her. He certainly should not have let her go to one of those personal growth workshops, which seemed to have filled her head with some strange notions of independence.

John, who had never had any physical ailments, began to experience serious stomach pains. His doctor diagnosed a fairly advanced ulcer, which called for surgical treatment. During his stay at the hospital, despite the many phone calls he made from his hospital bed, his investments registered dramatic losses. John had just lost a major portion of his assets. He could no longer maintain the rigid control he had had over everything and everyone for most of his life. He was on his way to his moment of truth.

◆   ◆   ◆

Monica is the general manager of a company that produces construction materials. Theoretically, she shares this responsibility with her husband. In actual fact, however, she is the one who looks after everything, since her husband, being somewhat of a schizoid type, does not have both feet on the ground, and dreams up projects without much practical sense. So she is the one who manages everything, at home and at work. She feels comfortable in this role. She plans, organises, and directs a staff of twenty people with a master's touch. At the beginning of her marriage, she had two children to whom she paid little attention, being too caught up in her many responsibilities. Yet she always made sure they had everything they needed, in material terms; they went to a good school and got a sound education. She is a responsible woman.

She has always taken care of herself physically. In the summers, she plays golf, her favourite sport. She enjoys evenings in fancy clubs where she has the opportunity to meet her kind of people. She is always very well dressed, in conservative yet elegant clothes. She is proud of her success, which she has earned through sheer grit and willpower.

Indeed, her life had started out as anything but a bed of roses. When she was eight years old, she had a terrible shock when her mother died. She had loved her very much, and this was a major loss that broke her heart, and something closed up in her so that she wouldn't feel this pain ever again. From that moment on, she decided that she was old enough to look after herself. She quit school at an early age and began to work in business. Being very resourceful, she ended up with interesting positions of responsibility. When she married, she had extensive experience in the business world, which allowed her to effectively take charge of her husband's company.

She had always had some minor health problems which she had easily overcome through sheer willpower, until one day she fell seriously ill and was diagnosed with cancer. She had to stop all professional activities and get medical help. At first, she adamantly resisted her illness. Yet she was smart, and she sought help. A therapist friend of hers assisted her through this process, and she eventually acknowledged her state. She saw how she had shut herself off from life for so long, since she was eight years old in fact. For her, this became an occasion for major awakening. She could have become even more rigid, yet on the contrary she was able to take this opportunity to reflect, to take stock of her life, and to realise that she was not invulnerable, indeed that vulnerability might perhaps be a quality. She opened up to her relatives and friends, and accepted their care. She let go of her need to control, and found herself better off for it. The energy of her soul re-emerged.

◆   ◆   ◆

This structure's defence system is insensitivity and strong mental control. The individual feels little or no emotions. Life is orchestrated by the mind, which has learned to develop its control mechanisms in all circumstances. The intellect is generally highly developed in order to foster this attitude. The heart is closed, cold, and everything happens at the mind level. Examples such as John and Monica give an idea of the kinds of behaviour that are typical of this structure. What past experiences could generate this kind of behaviour?

7-2 Past life experiences at the root of the rigid structure

This structure stems from a **powerful experience of emotional suffering that the individual has been unable to integrate**. At a time when the heart was open, and emotions were readily available, a situation arose that was so painful that one was unable to deal with the suffering. All sensitivity was then frozen, and the individual closed up in order not to feel. *Since the horse acted up in a way that bore too heavy a cost, it was simply bound up and left on the side of the road.*

During a session involving breath work, Bridget spontaneously reconnected with a past life that unfolded before her mind's eye with incredible clarity. This is what she had to say:

I am a man who is part of Spanish nobility around the 18th century. I am married to a woman of great beauty, Rosalia, whom I love more than anything in the world. She is not only beautiful but also intelligent, with the grace of a goddess and great musical talent. She loves me very much and we are very happy together. I can see us at a great reception given at my castle. She is there, dressed in a long brightly coloured gown, with her hair dressed on top of her head, resplendent in her beauty. I am so proud to be at her side! Then these images fade and I find myself at her bedside. She is sick with a disease that none of the doctors I have brought in from all corners of the kingdom have been able to diagnose or heal. My wife is dying. I cannot tolerate this. I am told of a healer who lives at a two-day walking distance from the castle, and who might be able to do something. I decide to go and fetch this man myself, and bring him back to the castle as soon as possible. On horseback, keeping a good pace, I should be able to make the trip in less than a day. As soon as I alight from my horse, I let him know of my request. At first, he is reticent, but as a result of my insistence and financial generosity, he finally agrees to come with me. The time he takes to prepare his remedies seems endless to me. Then we hastily depart. But as I mount my horse, a terrible anguish grips my throat, an intuition that I violently push away. Rosalia has just died. No, it can't be true! "Come on, healer, we are leaving on the double, we are in a hurry." We get to the castle a few hours later, I run to the bedroom without seeing anyone, I arrive at the bedside of my beloved. She is no longer breathing. She is dead. I can't believe it. Her mother and sister quietly enter the room, sadly nodding their heads. No, this is too painful. Then it is as if a block of ice fell in my heart. Nothing can ever make it warm again. My whole being becomes cold, my face becomes closed and my sensitivity is numbed so that I can no longer feel anything, or any pain. As the funeral is held, I speak to no one. My children are crying, but I don't care. I am as closed as the tomb that has now taken my beloved away from me, and thus I shall remain. I carry on with my life, a cold and distant individual. I no longer take care of my children, whom I have placed in the care of a governess. Thus I age with each passing year, becoming more and more taciturn and closed. I die with a firmly set resolve: "To love, to have an open heart, to have feelings, all this is very painful. From now on, I must never again feel anything, I must remain closed, so as to protect myself."

In her present life, Bridget is indeed caught in a rigid structure. She was very aware that something major was missing in her life, especially in her relationships. She hardly felt anything. She tried her best to keep love at bay, and emotional outpourings made her very ill at ease. Through her process of inner work, she was able to defuse this dynamic and recover a source of energy within herself that she had never experienced before, and that gave her once again the ability to love, to feel, and to live a vibrant life.

This is the story of a structure that was created as a result of a major heartache. Other types of experiences can also lead to such an emotional shut down: a young woman, who was also caught in a rigid structure, reconnected with a memory where, as a young girl, she had to witness her parents being tortured and then killed and thrown in a mass grave. She saw them laying dead in the great hole, on top of a pile of other corpses, after screaming under torture. It was too much: she had to block the pain in order to protect herself, and so she did. But she took this memory with her, and came back to this life with a heart of stone. How can we judge people for their behaviour, their coldness, their indifference, when we know that they have become this way as a result of too much suffering?

As is the case with other structures, there have been numerous occasions for this type of experience throughout the course of past lives. As we observe human history, with all its wars, its invasions, its incidents of collective or individual brutality, one can easily understand how the collective unconscious might be loaded with this type of defence system. Whether it takes the form of brutal separation of parents and/or children, or the unexpected loss of a cherished person (spouse, lover, child), or the horrible spectacle of torture or injustice being inflicted on loved ones—anything that goes beyond the limits of what is bearable—will lead to this kind of shut down. The common factor is the brutality of the emotional shock. It ultimately makes no difference whether the individual has personally experienced such situations, or included them in his personal baggage in resonance with the emotional charge stored in the collective unconscious. What matters is knowing that these memories are lodged in our unconscious, and that they must be deactivated in order to recover the totality of one's being and one's freedom to live life fully.

7-3 Present life experiences that foster the recreation of a rigid structure

A young child is very sensitive emotionally. He has just arrived from higher spheres of existence where he has recovered all the sensitivity of his soul. He is wide open and his emotional system is very receptive. He has not yet had the time to build or rebuild any particular defence system, until the day when some particular circumstance reactivates the memories. As with the other structures, it is not necessary for this to be a cataclysmic event.

In John's case, whose story was told at the beginning of this chapter, the rigid structure had been reactivated by several circumstances in his early childhood. One in particular can shed light on his reaction to the presence of the little cat in his house:

During the first years of his life, John lived with his parents on the outskirts of the city. He was brought up with a big dog, Amadeus, that his parents adopted when his grandmother died. This was not a young dog, but he was a great friend to John. They had a great time playing together, and John loved to fall asleep with his arms around the soft fur of the dog's neck.

John was seven years old when his parents had to move to the city. They found a really nice apartment in a large new building, which was exactly what they were looking for. There was just one problem: pets were not allowed in the building. No matter: the dog was old, and his health was faltering; he would simply be put to sleep. Not a word would be said to John about it, since he would make a scene. A few days before the move, while John was still at school, his parents took the dog to the SPCA. Back from school, John looked for his dog, and his parents explained the situation. When John understood that he would never again see his great friend, something in his chest collapsed. A pain so great overwhelmed him that his heart turned to ice so as not to feel it.

Following is another example of the type of conditions that foster the recreation of a rigid structure:

Ted and Josette have been living together for 5 years. They have two young children, Sydney, 3, and little Victor, 18 months. Their relationship gradually sours, until finally Josette decides to leave the household to go and live with a new boyfriend. She leaves with little Victor, while Sydney is left under Ted's care.

A week later, after the separation, Ted is to bring Josette the last of her personal belongings. When they get to the front of the house, Ted asks Sydney if he wants to go inside. The answer is yes. Josette is very tense, as her new relationship is already going sour. While Ted and Josette discuss certain material arrangements, Sydney plays with his younger brother, with whom he has just been reunited. Then it's time to go. Ted calls his son: "Come on, Sydney, we're going home". Sydney: "I'd like to stay here tonight". Sydney casts an inquiring look at his mother, to see whether she might agree to this. Her response is immediate, and very curt: "Out of the question!" (meaning: "I have enough on my plate already"). Sydney says nothing, receiving this rejection square in the face, loaded with all of his mother's impatient energy which, in fact, had noting to do with him directly. Yet he can't tell the difference. It hurts. He takes his dad's hand and they leave.

Some months later, during a conversation in the car. Ted asks Sydney: "Do you have a girlfriend?" – "No, I have three of them." – "Why three?" And Sydney answers: "If one of them leaves me, I still have the other two."

Sydney could have had a more emotional reaction to this childhood shock, thus reactivating more of a sense of abandonment. Yet, based on his memories, his response instead was to block the pain, which probably resonated with a painful experience in a more distant past. The defence system of calculating control was installed in order to "protect" him from further suffering of this type.

Sydney went on to become a lawyer. He is a handsome, intellectually bright man who is doing very well in his chosen profession. He remains a bachelor, as he doesn't see the point in getting entangled in emotional relationships. He is content to have a few regular mistresses, for some good occasional sex. Until one day, pressed by the power of his soul, he dared to open up his heart a little and face the pain he didn't integrate in his childhood (and probably in a more distant past).

It is easy to imagine a number of scenarios that can reactivate this type of memory and rebuild the initial rigid structure. This can take the form of violent situations, of course, which were experienced either personally, in the individual's present lifetime, or were witnessed by him (events in Bosnia or Iraq must have created a number of rigid structures in children and parents), or painful situations within one's own family: a father who beats the mother or the children, sexual abuse, etc. But even less spectacular situations can suffice, such as the death of a beloved grandmother, the prolonged absence of a father to whom one is very attached and who is gone on an extended journey, a divorce (as in the case of Sydney), the death of a brother or sister one felt very close to, or an apparently benign situation such as what happened with John's dog. As we have seen earlier, it takes very little to reactivate an active memory if it is already highly charged emotionally.

7-4 The Rigid Structure's Defence System

> ✓ **The underlying fear of the structure: fear of feeling, fear of emotional vulnerability, fear of losing control.**
>
> ✓ **Emotional charge: paralysed emotions, emotional insensitivity.**
>
> ✓ **Basic defence system:** emotional **shut-down,** mental rigidity and **control** through lower mind activity: wanting to be right, to dominate, narrow-mindedness.
>
> ✓ **Declaration of the structure:** "EVERYTHING IS UNDER CONTROL. I will feel nothing, don't come close to me, don't touch me."

• **Inner consequences of this defence system:**

One's **entire emotional capacity** is frozen. In addition, since the mechanism was installed as a result of an unexpected shock, the defence system generates **mental control** of one's environment so as never again to be taken by surprise or risk a re-emergence of feelings. The horse cannot be allowed any more unexpected moves, so it is carefully trussed up and left by the side of the road, and the coachman then comes down from his seat with a firm determination that, from now on, he will be the one to pull the cart. This way, one can be certain that one will not end up going all over the place. But one will also not get very far. All of one's behaviours will be conditioned by the fear of losing control.

While the psychopath is emotional and takes pleasure in being admired and popular, the rigid individual feels nothing. He doesn't want to feel. As far as he is concerned, feeling is a weakness, since his memories carry the constant message that "to feel is to get hurt". So **he thinks, calculates, and tries to foresee and plan** what will happen next, and he relies strictly on his own mental perceptions to direct the course of his life. The coachman has become the king of the road. He learns to become strong willed, but this will is made to serve the purpose of self protection (this will be a positive asset when he decides to transform his structure). He doesn't manipulate like a psychopath: **he directs, dominates and controls with a cool hand**.

7-5 Typical Behaviours of the Rigid Structure

1) General attitude towards life: control and mental rigidity

In this structure, we find the characteristics of the lower mind in its mental aspect, since all emotions are effectively blocked.

The emotional shutdown has led to an over-development of the mental aspect of the lower mind (see Chapter 4 of *Free Your True Self 2*, the strategies of the lower mind). We then find the following characteristics:

—A very rigid mental structure, always has to be right, narrow-mindedness.

—Often intellectually brilliant: as the mental energy is predominant, the child generally really enjoyed intellectual studies as they are presented in the western world. But this does not necessarily make him "intelligent", in the sense of open-mindedness, creativity and intuition.

—Functions strictly logically and analytically, with constant rationalisations: everything has to be explainable. Intuition, as far as he is concerned, is a weakness that must be treated with suspicion.

—A disciplined, systematic, predictable, organised lover of routine; lack of originality and creativity.

—Abhors change, improvisation, or surprises; everything has to be predictable and planned.

—Cold-blooded pride; sense of superiority stemming from the intellect.

—Denial or sublimation of any deep feeling.

—Emotions are controlled and rationalised.

—Materialism; being interested in material things allows one to avoid feelings.

—Stiffens at any emotional display of joy, love, gratitude, as well as grief or sadness.

—Is always very serious; one doesn't often laugh when one is caught in this structure, not because one is sad (one doesn't have such feelings) but because joy does not exist in the mechanism of the mind.

—Works alone and equates this isolation with self-reliance. Loathes groups, unless he is the one in charge, in which case he will remain very distant from the people under his orders or his direction, and will lead in an uncompromising, inflexible manner.

—**What a rigid personality hates and avoids most:** emotional demonstrations, hugs, groups, people, being touched (physically or emotionally), anything that might somehow strike an emotional cord, and anything that might require a more supple physical body (dance, demonstrations of physical exuberance).

2) Couple relationships, and relationships in general:

HEART OF STONE

A rigid structure will cut off all sensitivity within a personality, i.e. any openness to love. This emotionally numb state is quite different from that of a psychopath, who uses the warmth of love in order to seduce and manipulate people. A rigid personality blocks this energy, replacing it with a mental mechanism of domination and control. A psychopath dominates by recycling the energy of the heart for selfish purposes, while a rigid person dominates by using mental power.

In a relationship context, besides the general attitude described above, we note the following behaviours:

—Wants to control everything in the relationship, and will therefore be the **domineering** type; will tend to prefer partners with "dominated" type structures: masochist, oral, or schizoid.

—Deals with conflict through **logical arguments**, indifference and contempt.

—Communicates rationally and superficially; cannot express feelings.

—**Coldness**, insensitivity.

—Harshness, selfishness.

—**Pride**; despises others and coldly manipulates them.

—Calculating, distant.

—Cold fanaticism.

—Unlike a psychopath who tends to surround himself with people of the opposite sex in order to constantly maintain a court of admiring fans, rigid people, whether male or female, will tend to prefer the company of men. This is understandable since, from a cultural standpoint, men are encouraged and conditioned from early childhood to build a rigid structure.

—Family relationships: **authoritarian**, imposes his will in a harsh, direct manner; insensitive to demonstrations of affection, either from parents or from children; does not listen; often remains aloof (unless combined with a psychopath structure); loathes parties and gatherings where there is great fun and laughter.

Culturally speaking, as this kind of structure is encouraged in the education of boys (a man never cries, right?), we will find this structure mostly prevalent among men. There are also physical-energetic conditions linked to the sexual polarity of the physical body (metabolism, hormones, etc.), that tend to make people of the female gender closer to their emotions. If, at the moment of choosing an incarnation, one needs to experience a rigid structure, one will tend to choose a body of the male gender.

This is, of course, a very general viewpoint, as a great deal of rigidity can also be found among women. The rigid woman type is well known: the frigid, cantankerous shrew; the businesswoman wanting to play the businessman; the often rigid mother superior in a convent; the harsh, insensitive mother; the strict teacher the egotistical scientist infatuated with her role; the wealthy, haughty, cold heiress; etc. The fact that we find such caricatures in soap operas, not only of rigid people but of other structures as well, is due to the fact that they reflect a reality within the content of the present collective unconscious.

3) Sexuality

Very often, a rigid structure in a woman will translate into non-existent sexual relations, due either to lack of interest or to frigidity. This is easily understandable. During intercourse, a woman plays a rather "yin", receptive, sensitive, open role corresponding to her femininity. In order to achieve orgasm, one must be able to let go and to experience genuine surrender, and this is unbearable to a rigid structure.

On the other hand, a rigid man will have no problem with sex. He will make sure he remains in control and dominates the situation. He will have purely physical relations that are totally devoid of feeling. A typical attitude for a rigid man, right after intercourse, is not to look into his partner's eyes to tell her how beautiful she is and how he loves her (unless, by God's grace, the magic of love unhinged him at least momentarily from his structure). Instead, he will get up to read his newspaper, make an important phone call, or smoke a cigarette on his own thinking, most likely, of anything but what he has just experienced.

4) The physical body

• Body shape

Generally handsome and well proportioned. The energy is spread somewhat evenly throughout the body, with a lot of energy concentrated in the head.

• Health

A rigid person is "always" in good health, or so he claims, for two reasons: first of all, to admit that one is ill would be a sign of weakness and vulnerability. This is out of the question. He is proud and, though he may not need to project a spectacular image, as would a psychopath, he does however like to maintain an image of superiority and invulnerability. Secondly, he doesn't feel anything, so he doesn't feel the signs of a tired or suffering physical body. He manages his body as he manages his life: with his head, like a despot, on the basis of ideas rather than hunches or feelings.

For example, if he takes an interest in alternative healing techniques, he may decide to go on a prolonged fast after reading a book on the subject, although this may not necessarily appear to be appropriate for him; or he may decide to jog five miles a day, and he will do it, unlike other structures that lead a person to make decisions that they almost never put into practice. He will often be seen practising some form of sport, or body-building routine. So he is apparently capable of taking care of his physical body and following a particular discipline, which will become an asset when the structure becomes more flexible. Meanwhile, his lack of flexibility and sensitivity tends to make him hard on himself, as he is hard on everything around him. His will is hard and stiff, and his body will end up suffering the consequences of this. The rigid aspect of the personality may well lead to cigarette smoking. Indeed, emotions have the effect of causing blood vessels to dilate, while tobacco tends to make them contract. Instinctively, a rigid structure will tend to use this physical means to counteract any emergence of emotions.

When he does fall ill, it will tend to be all at once: the structure collapses. Everything has been repressed through an act of will, and placed under mental control, but at some point the body can no longer take the demands placed upon it: it becomes worn out and "breaks down". This generally takes time, and does not occur before the age of 50 to 55. What we see then is a whole spectrum of illnesses stemming from the stress required to keep everything under control, not just emotions, but also all the people around him, his work, projects, and finances.

There will also be illnesses stemming from inner rigidification, in order not to feel anything. Rigid people are stiff, and this stiffness permeates everything. We thus get illnesses affecting the bones (arthritis) or muscles, as well as stomach ulcers and heart attacks resulting from excessive demands placed upon the body and the nervous system.

When illness finally does occur, the individual feels extremely lost, since he has never learned to ask for help. He becomes vulnerable and dependent, something he always strove to avoid at all cost. This is a very painful experience, but it can be an excellent opportunity for a number of realisations. If the individual resists and hangs onto his rigidity despite the sorry state of his physical body, he will give himself no chance of healing, and will carry his rigidity and his suffering along with him to the grave.

• Automatic choices in clothing

External appearance is important to a rigid individual. Yet unlike the psychopath who pays a great deal of attention to clothing in order to be seen, a rigid person will dress well, in elegant yet conservative, conventional, "businesslike" attire, in order not to cause any reaction. He does not want to reveal anything about himself, unlike the psychopath who likes to strut his stuff. His clothes must not attract attention and must maintain a certain distance between himself and others.

5) The energy aspect

The energy system related to this structure seems balanced, and one does not perceive any excess energy in certain places. On the other hand, this energy is noticeably low in colour and vibration, and it is static. This, in fact, reflects what is going on at the consciousness level. There is, however, intense activity at the level of the head, especially the forehead. Rigid people are driven by willpower.

The energy is cold, controlled, and it does not mix with other people's energy. This lack of radiance stems from an altogether different source when compared to that of a masochist. In the masochist structure, energy is compacted, compressed and kept congealed by a sense of powerlessness, by rage and by anger. Here, there is no question of feeling. Everything is controlled by the mind which will simply never allow any energy to radiate from the heart.

6) Relating to the material world and money

A rigid individual is usually successful in material and financial matters. He manages his budget in a very organised fashion, looks ahead, makes plans and calculations, leaving nothing to chance. His house, his car, and all of his possessions are clean, tidy, and kept in order. A rigid person's kitchen, for example, is a model of spotlessness and organisation, along with every other room in the house. His lifestyle is generally very conventional.

7) Relating to power

Both the rigid and the psychopath structures are interested in power, but for different reasons. In this structure where the defence system is based on control, one will tend to **seek power for purposes of control**. To be loved or admired is of little importance; a rigid individual does not need an audience. He might even be hated, this will not bother him, as long as he has the power and remains in control of the situation. He **imposes his will in a harsh, stiff manner**. He is neither flexible nor accommodating, and pleasing others is the last thing on his mind. He is often found in positions of power, perhaps in the company of psychopaths, but their behaviour is quite different. Working discreetly and in the background does not bother him, as long as he is the one pulling the strings.

8) Work

Rigid people are not often found in jobs that require human relationships. They do not seek to relate to people, since this has proven to be so painful in the past. They would rather work alone or in a context involving other rigid individuals, where everyone tacitly plays the same game.

Rigid people usually do well in business, where feelings have no place and are in fact unwelcome; discipline, willpower, emotional self-control are their assets. A striking image of a space full of rigid people at work would be a photograph of the main floor at the New York Stock Exchange. No other structure besides the rigid structure could stand this kind of work (for a while at least).

There will be many rigid people in the armed forces, preferably among the higher echelons. The level of organisation and discipline, the low level of importance given to feelings, the authoritarian hierarchy of power, all of these aspects really suit this structure.

Rigid people will also be found in all disciplines where the mind is activated and human contacts are expendable. Computers are a rigid person's paradise, as there is no risk of emotional confrontation with a computer monitor. They will also find work as administrative directors, organisers, planners and accountants.[1]

Politics can also be attractive to rigid individuals. If the rigid structure is predominant, they would rather stay behind the scene, as advisors and as the "power behind the throne". If the structure is combined with a psychopath structure, they will be in the forefront, using their psychopathic characteristics to address the public, and their rigid features to deaden the pain of setbacks.

Today's society is well suited for rigid individuals, as it allows them to achieve material "success", the kind of success that eventually ends up carrying a very high price tag, and is not the true mark of a successful life.

9) Service

Rigid personalities are either totally closed to any kind of service, or they will take part in charity work as an expression of social duty rather than an activity motivated by sympathy.

10) Pitfalls in spiritual seeking

If they happen to be interested in spiritual work, rigid people will gravitate towards activities requiring regular discipline, as well as ascetic disciplines where one's emotional reality can easily be repressed under the guise of sublimation (for example, Judeo-Christian asceticism, or Japanese Zen style asceticism). These disciplines have their purpose and can be excellent if used consciously and freely. Zen meditation, for example, can be a genuine path towards the liberation of the lower mind and towards genuine self-realisation. But unless one is vigilant, these approaches can easily be reclaimed by the ego. A rigid individual can easily meditate every day for years, thus remaining comfortably ensconced in his head. But the heart remains cold and no connection with the soul can take place since emotional blockages have merely been repressed instead of unravelled. Even if the structure can use such disciplines to develop a certain level of mastery and willpower, an essential element will still be lacking, due to the limitations of the structure. On the other hand, once transformation has occurred, certain characteristic qualities will remain, particularly a very centred, very strong will. In addition, if the individual is sincere and courageous in his approach to spiritual work, his soul will sooner or later attract circumstances which will allow him to correct the limited aspects of his practice.

11) Some practical suggestions and tasks leading to transformation

Even though they may never admit it and are unaware of the fact, rigid individuals are in great pain, as their psyche is very sensitive. They have had to become rigid in order to protect themselves. Behind this hard outer shell, there is a highly sensitive being. He doesn't feel anything anymore, but his soul suffers and waits for the necessary healing to occur so that it can once again express its sensitivity.

For this reason, it is once again important to stress that one should refrain from judging anyone, as we pointed out in the case of other structures. Rigid people need human warmth, and a demonstration of the joy of warm-hearted love. They need to heal past wounds so that, little by little, they can dare to love again. When this happens, the process becomes very beautiful, as I have witnessed many times during my sessions. For the rigid structure is not a complex one to dismantle (unlike the psychopath structure). This requires tact and a lot of love, but it can be done, and we may then witness all the sensitivity and inner beauty of the person, which had remained hidden under the hardened shell.

When one is caught in a rigid structure, one will need to practice the following steps, **with a great deal of gentleness**:

    —re-learn to **open up**, at the levels of the heart and mind;

    —be more attentive to others and develop one's relationships;

    —rediscover the benefits of gentleness and tenderness;

—work on becoming more open-minded with regard to new ways of seeing things; readings and conferences can be used to broaden one's viewpoints;

—eliminate criticism and judgement, and stop trying to always be right;

—relinquish control in order to gain mastery;

—learn to listen to others, and to welcome their differences;

—learn to experience the benefits of relaxation; listen to tapes of soft music and guided relaxation;

—welcome the unexpected and create occasions for surprises; learn not to plan ahead so much;

—make faces in the mirror each morning for one minute;

—stop taking oneself so seriously, **learn to laugh again**, to play; reconnect with the child within;

—allow oneself to be taken care of and pampered through massages; learn to let go;

—dress casually;

—work on developing physical and psychological **flexibility**: dancing (tap dancing), singing, and non-structured activities will be beneficial;

—dare to feel and to love again.

Once transformed, this structure offers marvellous qualities.

7-6 The Rigid Structure Transformed

Emotional mastery is one of the great qualities this structure stands to gain, once it has been transformed. Rigid people who have reclaimed their sensitivity will know how to remain simple, respectful and discreet in their emotional demonstrations. Instead of repressing emotions, they welcome them and keep them in check in the light of their soul. Thus, a transformed rigid structure generates **genuine sensitivity**, without sentimentality or mushiness.

This translates into the ability to remain calm, balanced and objective, no matter what the circumstances may be. So what we have is a person who is both very sensitive and very **centred**, flexible yet very solid. In our emotionally supercharged society, this person may still be judged as being cold, when he or she is in fact just not interested in playing the kind of emotional game in which most people are caught up. The apparent insensitivity of a transformed rigid structure is very different, in terms of its source, from the insensitivity of a rigid individual who is caught in his structure. The latter stems from refusing to feel anything and systematically shutting out the world, while the apparent insensitivity of the transformed structure comes from being consciously in the here and now, and reacting with appropriate sensitivity while refusing to waste energy in futile emotional turmoil.

The intellect, which is usually highly developed in this structure, generates a high degree of mental clarity that is no longer limited by the rigidity of the structure, as well as a great deal of open-mindedness resulting from its transformation.

A transformed rigid individual will put his **strong willpower** to work on concrete contribution projects. He will be an excellent organiser, since he is now able to be sensitive to the human aspect without making a big deal of it, while retaining a strong mental structure. This will make him a good negotiator, different from a transformed psychopath, yet no less effective.

He will not be afraid to take risks, and can become an inspiration in support of great causes. As fear is essentially an emotional mechanism, it is easy for him to bring it under control. **Courage, valour, heroism** will be among his qualities. He becomes an inspiration as he helps others reach beyond their limitations, develop their willpower, and defuse their fears. There is also a great deal of **purity in sentiment**, a lot of **energy**, genuine **nobility**, natural **detachment** and great **respect for other people's autonomy and freedom**. A transformed rigid individual has the soul of a true hero, of the kind we see in the movies: **brave, centred, relaxed**, never loses his cool even in the most critical situations, **sensitive** yet not excessively so, on appropriate occasions. He has a high level of **integrity, intelligence, and intuitiveness**, is comfortable in his physical body.[2] At present, due to our collective conditioning, we are most often shown a transformed rigid structure in male form. But things are changing fast, and people who have chosen a female body now have the opportunity to develop all of the qualities of this structure just as men do. The world is full of brave female heroes, who are centred, solid on their feet, intelligent, and who, shoulder to shoulder with men of quality, are making a valuable contribution and a positive difference in the world.

• Declaration of transformation

> I celebrate my sensitivity, I am able to let go,
> I dare to love.
> I am able to feel emotions, and to experience them fully,
> with a high level of mastery and authenticity.

• Contribution task

To stand as an example of willpower, courage, centredness and mastery, as someone who is able to extend his limits in order to take part in building a new world of peace and justice.

7-7 The Rigid Structure – Summary

• **Basic fear of the structure:** fear of feeling, fear of losing control, fear of being vulnerable.

• **Source experiences in the past:** intense emotional shock leading to loss of sensitivity and a closing up of the personality.

• **Defence system:** control, domination, coldness, arrogance, pride.

• **Declaration of the defence system:** "EVERYTHING IS UNDER CONTROL, I don't feel anything."

• **Work to be done:** recover one's sensitivity, vulnerability, flexibility, be willing to experience emotions again (one's own as well as other people's), dare to love.

• **Declaration of transformation:**

> I welcome my emotions, and I experience them fully.

• **Fundamental qualities of the soul to be recovered:**

> Sensitivity, flexibility.

• **Qualities of the structure:** WILLPOWER, CENTEREDNESS, EMOTIONAL SELF-CONTROL, courage, heroism, purity in sentiment, lots of energy, detachment, integrity, courageous defender of freedom and justice.

• **Contribution task:**

> Be an example of willpower and courage, dare to take risks to save the planet.

Way to go, you rigid folks, now let's dance!

---

[1] See films such as The Game, The Bodyguard, and Pretty Woman for typical examples of this structure going through a de-rigidification process, for the enjoyment of the audience.

[2] We have a typical example of a transformed hero in Wallace, the hero in the film Braveheart.

chapter 8

General Overview of the Five Structures

This is a comparative summary of some aspects of the various structures; the various points addressed are:

1 The structure's declaration of self-defence
2 Characteristic fear
3 Relationships
4 Manipulation techniques
5 Attitudes in the face of conflict
6 The physical body:
    —appearance
    —dress
    —how the defence system uses the body
7 Energy characteristics
8 Dominant-dominated / perpetrator-victim
9 Relating to the material world
10 Power
11 Pitfalls in spiritual seeking
12 How are you doing? – Automatic responses
13 What each structure hates most
14 Typical occupations
15 How each structure can be manipulated
16 Mind/emotions interface
17 Specific qualities of the soul to be recovered
18 Declaration of transformation
19 Some of the qualities that emerge when the structure is transformed
20 Structures in relation to rays

1) The structure's declaration of self defence:

Schizoid: I'm out of here.
Oral: More.
Masochist: I am suffering and it's all your fault.
Psychopath: Love me, I am special.
Rigid: Everything is under control.

2) Characteristic fear:

Schizoid: fear of life, fear of involvement.
Oral: fear of deprivation, fear of being abandoned.
Masochist: fear of being taken, fear of power.
Psychopath: fear of not being loved, of betrayal.
Rigid: fear of feeling, fear of losing control.

3) Relationships:

Schizoid: absent heart
Oral: hungry heart
Masochist: stifled heart
Psychopath: selfish, conceited heart
Rigid: heart of stone

4) Manipulation techniques:

Schizoid: withdraws.
Oral: demands, sticks like glue.
Masochist: makes the other feel guilty for his/her suffering.
Psychopath: seduces, performs, seeks to impress, lies.
Rigid: imposes his/her will.

5) Attitudes in the face of conflict:

Schizoid: withdrawal.
Oral: compensates through stuffing; hangs on and demands even more.
Masochist: submission or rebellion, blame, sabotage.
Psychopath   seduction, lies, deceit.
Rigid: cold reasoning; is always right.

6) The physical body
• body shape:

Schizoid   Oral   Masochist   Psychopath   Rigid

- **dress:**

Schizoid:	of little importance, or original and eccentric.
Oral:	has a closet overstocked with clothes
Masochist:	uncomfortable clothing.
Psychopath:	original, flashy clothes.
Rigid:	quality clothes, classic and conventional style.

- **eventual use of the physical body by the defence system:**

Schizoid:	soft drugs in order to disconnect from reality.
Oral:	lots of food.
Masochist:	has liver attacks…, injuries.
Psychopath:	alcohol, use of hard drugs (stimulants).
Rigid:	tobacco.

7) Energy characteristics:

Schizoid:	faded energy – gets tired quickly.
Oral:	heavy, sticky energy, quickly drains one's energy.
Masochist:	compact, sad energy – great ability to withstand fatigue depending on mindset.
Psychopath:	intrusive energy, hyperactivity that momentarily boosts one's level of endurance.
Rigid:	cold energy – great endurance, does not feel fatigue.

8) Dominant/dominated:

Schizoid:	dominated.
Oral:	mixed: dominant when it comes to taking, yet dominated when dependent.
Masochist:	dominated.
Psychopath:	dominant.
Rigid:	dominant.

9) Relating to the world of money:

Schizoid:	disconnected from the material world.
Oral:	stuffing, tendency to accumulate.
Masochist:	overwhelmed my material responsibilities, poverty.
Psychopath:	uses material things to boost image.
Rigid:	material control.

10) Power
Schizoid: not interested, disconnected from his/her own power, while ignoring other people's power.

Oral: not interested, unless it brings physical or emotional food, or to dominate or enslave the providing source.

Masochist: powerlessness – does not recognise his/her own power, undermines other people's power; submission or rebellion.

Psychopath: seeks power in order to gain fame, love and recognition.

Rigid: seeks power in order to remain in control.

11) Pitfalls in spiritual seeking:
Schizoid: tends to disconnect even more from physical reality.

Oral: seeks a group or a master as a provider of energy, as a form of emotional compensation.

Masochist: chooses difficult paths and disciplines in order to suffer more and blame others.

Psychopath: uses psychic powers; seeks an audience among spiritual groups; charismatic false guru.

Rigid: chooses ascetic disciplines that provide a justification for emotional blockage.

12) How are you doing? – Automatic responses:
Schizoid: vague, confused response, or no response at all.

Oral: "Not very well. There's something I need that I'm not getting…"

Masochist: "Not well at all."

Psychopath: "Good, never better; life is extraordinary, and so am I."

Rigid: "I'm fine."

13) What each structure hates the most:
Schizoid: hates to be asked to get involved.

Oral: loathes all forms of discomfort and deprivation.

Masochist: hates authority, and happy people.

Psychopath: cannot stand criticism, and hates to be confronted with someone better, or better loved, than him.

Rigid: hates surprises, and anything that is at odds with his viewpoint; cannot stand emotional demonstrations and people who are in tune with their feelings.

14) Typical occupations:

Let us not forget that all structures can be found in any type of occupation, and when one practices a given occupation, this does not mean that one is caught in a corresponding structure. Yet the characteristic features of certain types of occupation can be reclaimed more easily than others by different structures. For example:

Schizoid: philosopher, computer technician or programmer, little
                known artist; unstable, eccentric occupations.
Oral: store owner, massage therapist...
Masochist: nurse, therapist in centres for people in crisis situations
                or people experiencing various forms of deep suffering...
Psychopath: highly popular artist, salesperson, lawyer, doctor, politician,
                guru...
Rigid: military officer, accountant, public servant, financier, business
                person, background politician...

15) Structures can be manipulated by nurturing specific areas of hope for each structure, or by reactivating certain aspects:

Schizoid: anticipation of easily achieved security, without involvement.
Oral: anticipation of stuffing – activating the fear of deprivation.
Masochist: anticipation of revenge – activating anger and the sense of
                injustice.
Psychopath: anticipation of fame and love – compliments.
Rigid: need for power and control – conceding that he is right.

16) Mind/emotions interface:

Depending on the structure, the "kama-mana" (the lower mind in relation to the emotional body) is more strongly activated in its emotional or mental aspect:

Schizoid: mental activity, emotional vulnerability and lightness.
Oral: emotional heaviness.
Masochist: emotional.
Psychopath: emotional.
Rigid: mental.

17) Specific qualities of the soul to be recovered:

Schizoid: capacity for concrete achievements.
Oral: fulfilment.
Masochist: joy and power of the soul.
Psychopath: true love, humility, integrity.
Rigid: sensitivity, flexibility.

18) Declaration of transformation:

Schizoid: I exist.
Oral: I am fulfilled.
Masochist: I am free, I have joy in my heart.
Psychopath: I am genuinely able to love.
Rigid: I can feel, and I adapt.

19) Some of the qualities that emerge when the structure is transformed:

Schizoid: creativity, intuition, impersonality, lightness of being.
Oral: generosity, abundance, fulfilment, pleasure to be alive.
Masochist: compassion, service, support.
Psychopath: ability to confer power and to inspire others; integrity, dynamism.
Rigid: courage, centredness, mastery.

20) Structures in relation to rays

For those who are familiar with the seven rays' approach as presented by Alice Bailey, one can see the personality rays that are in tune with the various structures (remember that the more evolved a person is, the more the qualities of the structure and of the rays are evident):

Schizoid: third (abstraction), fourth (creativity) and sixth (because of the religious aspect); rarely the first, fifth and seventh, because of the concrete manifestation of these rays.
Oral: predominance of even numbered rays.
Masochist: even numbered rays, especially the sixth (fanaticism or compassion).
Psychopath: second (because of the relationship and popularity seeking aspect); sixth, and fourth (because of their manifestation of originality); they will more rarely be found on the third and fourth rays, as these do not promote relationships.
Rigid: all the odd numbered rays, especially the first (because of the link with non emotional power) and the seventh (because of the organisation aspect).

chapter 9

Combinations of Structures

There are many pitfalls to be avoided on the road to transformation, and there is often a great deal of confusion. This stems, at least in part, from the fact that the structures carry different, and often opposite types of problems. Gurdjieff emphasised this contradictory aspect of the human psyche:

> Man (at the personality level) does not have an individual "Self". Instead, there are hundreds and thousands of little separate "selves", which are most often unaware of each other, have no relation to each other, or may in fact be hostile, exclusive and incompatible with one another.[1]

How do we cope with this inner chaos?[2]

Knowing our inner dynamics according to each structure is a good start towards becoming more aware of the way we function. But, knowing that the ego is conditioned by the totality of these five structures, which are active to varying degrees in each individual, we realise how complex the work of transformation can be. To illustrate this complexity, here are some comments regarding several combinations of structures.

9-1 The masochist-psychopath combination: rage, anger, manipulation, problem with power.

The work required seems to be contradictory:

—psychopath: self-centred, false identity, must recover his/her true identity through **humility**;

—masochist: stifled identity, must recover his/her identity through **self-affirmation**.

Both structures refer directly to a problem of non-identity, or false identity, in relation to power.

As the masochist structure was being developed, the ego was stifled, negated, rejected, and it experienced a profound sense of powerlessness and non-recognition. This triggered a genuine experience of **loss of identity**, with a lot of rage and anger.

As the psychopath structure was being developed, the ego learned that to be itself was not enough to be loved, and that in order to be recognised, one had to behave in such a way as to please others. So there again, there was a denial of one's essential being and the loss of a natural and wholesome sense of identity.

In both cases, the true identity of one's being was denied. If one is caught in this double structure, the inner work to be done will not be easy. Indeed, in order to get out of the masochist dynamic, one must learn self-affirmation by recovering the capacity to express oneself freely. Yet once this wholesome process has been initiated, there is a good chance that it will be reclaimed by the psychopath structure, which will use it as a justification for attention getting and approval seeking, ultimately fostering a false sense of self-affirmation and encouraging a manipulative use of power. The psychopath needs to work on humility, while the masochist needs to free himself from bondage…a rather difficult task!

In addition, both structures reinforce each other in terms of **rebellion**: an active masochist rebels in order to counteract the sense of being stifled, while a psychopath rebels because he wants to be the only one holding the reins of power.

The fear of others (fear of debasement and fear of betrayal) is also reinforced. Both structures lead to a high degree of isolation from others. When the masochist dynamic is active, one seeks approval because one is afraid of being stifled and manipulated by others. When the psychopath structure is active, one seeks approval because one is afraid of not being loved enough. Both mechanisms are very similar and mutually reinforcing. The fear of others translates into repressed anger and aggression in the case of the masochist structure, and into manipulative, seductive and dominating energy in the case of the psychopath structure. So in this case, there is an inner mix of energies that leads an individual to profoundly loathe others (for everything they "did to him"), yet he must please them and gain some form of influence over them. So he covers up the anger with a seductive, generous, radiating outer appearance, as if he was love personified. These are two structures that are very hard to live with internally. Sooner or later, the individual caves in, without knowing why.

9-2 The masochist-rigid combination: inward withdrawal, frustration, stiffness, anger, judgement, wanting to be right.

In the rigid structure, one wants to control everything, to make sure things go their way and people behave in accordance with their decisions. Right there, we have a good starting point from which to generate the frustration and dissatisfaction associated with the masochist structure. Indeed, as the latter is constantly looking for reasons to relive its deep-seated inner dissatisfaction, it will use all the demands and the inflexibility of the rigid structure as a basis for judging others as being bad, evil, and generally not "on the level", and complain about everything that does not match its own standards. The pride and lack of flexibility of the rigid structure is thus combined with the resistance to life and to others that characterises the masochist structure, to nurture a profound dissatisfaction about everything. This combination thus reinforces not only the inner dissatisfaction of the masochist structure, but also the judgmental attitude of the rigid structure: I am an all right person (on the level), but others are not. In addition, the inwardly locked up aspect of the rigid structure fosters withdrawal and non-communication. In this way, the masochist structure can stay in its corner and wordlessly nurture all of its frustrations, for a good long while. Stomach ulcers are bound to develop.

This double dynamic is difficult to work on, since getting out of it means working apparently in two opposite directions:

Indeed, the masochist dynamic compels the individual to bow (or to rebel) in the face of authority. He will thus need to try to recover his capacity for unhampered self-expression, the capacity for self-affirmation without fear (passive masochist) and without aggressiveness (active masochist), no longer being afraid to speak his truth, in an attitude of peace, light heartedness and happy detachment.

On the other hand, the rigid structure compels the ego to affirm itself in a stiff, unilateral manner, to want to be right at all times, to steadfastly hold onto one's viewpoint, to try to control and to dominate any given situation. The work that needs to be done in this case is to develop flexibility, to get rid of this false self-affirmation, to learn to let go of one's viewpoints in order to really listen to others, to consider other people's opinions and make the mind more supple, open and able to change. This seems like a move in the opposite direction from that of the masochist structure, where the emphasis is on building strength (the true strength of the soul) in order to have the courage to express and manifest one's viewpoints.

Much of the confusion arising in the course of working on one's ego stems from the fact that one has not clearly defined the source of one's problems. Teaching a rigid individual to stick up for himself and hold onto his viewpoints will quickly be reclaimed by the structure, which will merely use it as a form of reinforcement. Teaching a masochist individual to respect another person's viewpoint can also be misused by the structure, since for eons he has bowed before others out of fear.

One must develop the right level of self-affirmation and respect for others, while being extremely vigilant so that the ego does not use fine theories to end up nurturing and reinforcing its own structures. This must be done by consciously choosing a state of inner **contentment** that is not dependent on circumstances, while consciously and intensively practising an attitude of **good will** (an effective antidotes for both structures). **Practising humour and avoiding the tendency to overdramatise** also really help to alleviate both aspects.

9-3 The oral-psychopath combination: maximum energy pumping.

The oral and psychopath structures combined within one individual are mutually reinforcing. Both are played out in the area of relationships, trying to draw energy from other people, to counteract the sense of deprivation and abandonment (oral) and to feed the false self (psychopath). The two mechanisms demand eternal love, and experience "abandonment" as a deeply wounding event. Under such conditions, relationships cannot help but be alienating, since both structures seek to dominate others in order to secure their energy supply. In the context of intimate relationships, this creates "dominant vs. dominated" dynamics, which are heavily emotionally charged with manipulations, expectations and fears. Sex is a favourite field of activity for this combination of structures, which uses this type of exchange to draw a maximum amount of energy from the other partner. The individual is always "on the make", looking for a partner.

9-4 The oral-masochist combination: guaranteed lifelong dissatisfaction.

When these two structures inhabit a single individual, they reinforce each other's dissatisfaction. The oral aspect makes the individual constantly dissatisfied, and this dissatisfaction is reclaimed by the masochist structure to confirm that life is no picnic and people are mean.

9-5 The schizoid-masochist combination: failure and non-manifestation.

The two structures have a deep fear of self-manifestation, for different, mutually reinforcing reasons. The schizoid structure results in an incapacity to carry out any concrete project successfully, and the masochist structure uses this to nurture a sense of powerlessness and to blame everyone.

◆ ◆ ◆

These are just a few examples illustrating the challenges awaiting those engaged in inner work. Yet one must remember that these structures are merely components of our instrument, and that we are also equipped to make them evolve. These structures are not our true nature, and we do not have to remain caught in them for all eternity. As soon as we realise their presence within us, and are determined to transform them, each of us has every inner resource needed to find his/her way back to the seat of the soul.

[1] Ouspensky, *In Search of the Miraculous: Fragments of an Unknown Teaching*. New York: Harcourt, Brace.
[2] The approach used in Psychosynthesis focuses in particular on this aspect of our makeup, defining the "self" as an aggregate of "sub-personalities". An excellent approach created by Roberto Assagioli, it fosters an integration and unification of these contradictory aspects, thus opening the gates to the energy of the soul.

chapter 10

On Our Way to Freedom

Human beings cannot be fully understood unless we consider the evolutionary process in which we are involved. Without this perspective, the human condition is of such inextricable complexity that it defies understanding; otherwise the descriptions we have of how humans function remain partial and unsatisfactory.

On the other hand, if we consider the evolutionary process in light of the teachings of the Ageless Wisdom, along with the most recent observations in modern psychology, we find descriptive models of much greater substance, that are also far more relevant to our present human reality and to the practical problems that need to be solved in order to harmonise our inner world as well as the outer world.

This knowledge of the basic mechanisms of the unconscious, as we have just described them, will be very useful and can even prove to be a very powerful tool for inner healing, paving the way to genuine freedom, if **we see it in the context of the human evolutionary process** instead of a static condition in which we are caught, without a clue as to why that is, and which we need to get out of as quickly as possible.

10-1 Clearing the Path

As mentioned previously, these automatic defence systems had their purpose at a specific time in human evolution. They provided momentary protection at times of suffering, times of great physical or psychological stress. Without them, the ego could not have survived, and our instrument would have been destroyed. This mode of functioning was designed as part of the human evolutionary plan, and is still active in our present reality. But the evolutionary plan is moving us along, and times are changing.[1]

As time goes by, our inner Self, or soul, is awakening, and its influence is being felt more and more acutely. Thus, at a certain level of consciousness resulting from all of his past experiences, a human being develops more inner strength and more openness to the presence of his Higher Self, though without necessarily noticing it. This happens spontaneously the way a fruit ripens over time, according to natural law. This is when **these rigid systems of self-protection** go from being helpful to being impediments to fulfilment. For **our Higher Self, with its strength, wisdom and intelligence, wishes to gradually replace these automatic systems** that are programmed for our survival with another way of functioning which will enable us to express the full richness of our being, our creative power, our love. This higher consciousness, which is more and more active, not only knows full well how to "protect" us (obviously it wants to protect its instrument), and is able to do that very effectively if we just get out of its way, but it also becomes a **reliable guide**, available at any moment of our lives, as well as the driving force behind the free expression of who we truly are.

Here we can go back to the analogy where the development of the personality[2] is likened to building a home where the Master—our Self—will eventually take up residence. Even though our personality is in fact not yet completed (since we are not yet at the point of living in a state of total well being and permanent harmony), nevertheless our life experiences, as they become more and more conscious, will generate an increasing inner urge to perfect this home.

The rigidified parts of the defence systems we have just described are like the raw materials and temporary means used at the construction stage: scaffolds, mechanical equipment and any other materials needed for the completion of the work. The building site is littered with empty paint cans and debris, which is normal for a house under construction. Yet we must bear in mind that, under this apparent chaos, a fine home will eventually emerge for the Master—our inner Self—to come and spread Light and Love in our world.

Indeed there comes a time when the house is ready and solid enough so that we can remove what is no longer useful. That is when we naturally feel the need to clear away all this clutter in order to be able to fully and freely enjoy our beautiful home. That is the point at which we want to clear away the limited, rigidified aspects of our personality in order to finally enjoy the beauty and richness of all that we've built internally over centuries of learning.

When our primary defence systems are ready to soften and fall away, **all that is left is the wealth of experience that makes our personality a unique instrument, with its own vibrant beauty**, a reflection of the beauty of our soul.

This is the point of evolution where a large number of people are at these days, and these are the people for whom the knowledge presented here is intended.

10-2 Witnessing: A Transformative Vantage Point

Being aware of the content of our unconscious can remain a purely intellectual form of knowledge, in which case it will not make much difference in our lives. However if we know how to put this knowledge to practical use in our day-to-day lives, it can be of great benefit both inwardly, in terms of healing and well being, and outwardly, especially in our relationships with others, as we will see further on.

Our ability to use this knowledge appropriately will depend first of all on our ability to practice **the witness stance**. This attitude has been recommended in every genuine spiritual discipline. It has also been called other names: mindfulness, self-awareness, etc. It is an inner attitude, a deliberate positioning of our awareness that enables us, among other things, **to observe our personality in action**, every waking moment of our lives. This observation should be carried out in a very loving, compassionate and even humorous way towards ourselves, **staying especially clear of any judgmental self-talk**. A witness is not a judge!

This quiet observation allows us to distance ourselves from our inner mechanisms, and this in itself is a major step towards transformation.

It is the first fundamental step towards what is called **non-identification with ego**, non-identification with the reactions of our three bodies, particularly our emotional and mental reactions (followed by those of the physical body). Non-identification does not mean denial or repression. It means acknowledging what is there, so as to be more aware of the potential malfunctions of our instrument, and as much as possible not to let our lives be automatically governed by old defence patterns that have become inadequate. We thus have the opportunity to be more closely connected with our instrument, getting to know it better, and being able to carry out repairs and improvements more effectively.

This fosters the presence of a loving, intelligent higher consciousness within us, which helps us stay more centred and more stable. It also enables us little by little to base our actions on a deeper understanding and wisdom rather than on automatic reactions. Non-identification with our ego allows us to develop the habit of acting out of higher consciousness; but this must be done with **a great deal of patience, gentleness and love towards ourselves**. If we see our mechanisms taking over, that's OK, there is no need to get all worked up over it. We simply become more aware that we have some issues to work on, to heal, to liberate within us, and we will take appropriate measures to do so.

• Taking responsibility for our emotional states

Practising the witness stance enables us, among other things, to **take full responsibility for our emotional states**. Most often we tend to blame the world and the people around us for the problems we encounter and the unpleasant feelings arising within us. When life gets tough (the house gets uncomfortable), we usually think other people are the cause of our troubles. This does nothing to improve the house, and simply locks us into that uncomfortable state. On the other hand, as we grow to higher levels of awareness, whenever we encounter discomfort in our house (negative or painful emotional responses), instead of blaming others for drafts, we find out where those drafts come from and we get busy weatherproofing doors and windows.

This attitude of taking responsibility for our reactions is a real blessing, as it sets us free from emotional dependency and from the grip of inadequate emotional reactions, and hands us back our rightful power.[3] It is an excellent form of spiritual training on a daily basis.

10-3 Towards a Free, Meaningful and Joyful Life

When we use the witness stance from an evolutionary perspective, it allows us to understand and accept who we are with our strengths and weaknesses, our shadow and our light. In this sense, it is not necessary to reach the highest level of enlightenment or sainthood to enjoy a creative, dynamic, joyful and loving life.

1) Goodbye guilt and shame

Why be ashamed or blame ourselves for not being perfect? It's only normal since we are "under construction".

Many spiritual and moral teachings have extolled the beauty of the completed home (a personality that stands for the highest of values), which is great as a way to encourage us to try to achieve that. But all too often we were not given **the reason for our present so-called imperfection**, along with practical, concrete means of achieving that perfect state. Most importantly, we were not told that **this "imperfection" is perfect in itself**, since only by going through these intermediate states will we finally attain the ultimate state of perfection, of total inner liberation (the same way a cake that is still a mass of dough is perfect as it is, even though it does not look good or edible yet. Given time, it will be baked to perfection and good enough to eat). In fact, we were often made to feel more or less guilty because we still had a few residual traces of anger, jealousy, emotional dependency, pride, fear or any other inability to manifest what is most beautiful within us. In the old days, we even talked of "sin", and there are still shades of that guilt-ridden vision in the collective unconscious which continue to poison our lives.

• Dropping Resistance

This attitude of guilt, blame, and therefore non-acceptance makes us resist our building "leftovers" or unfinished parts. In this unfinished, uncomfortable house, each structure has its own way of putting up resistance. The schizoid structure leaves the house and goes wandering elsewhere dreaming or carrying on about the ideal house; the oral structure piles up more and more stuff inside the house; the masochist structure lays crumpled up in a corner wailing over its fate, and complaining to anyone within earshot, invariably blaming some guilty perpetrator for this situation; the psychopathic structure puts up a nice front, covers up whatever remains unfinished with lots of drapes, and does its best to draw attention whenever visitors come by so that nothing unfinished can possibly be noticed; the rigid structure simply sets up a computer on a workstation in some corner of the house.

But the truth is that we are really quite uncomfortable in this house. We often resist the way things are because we simply cannot figure out why we are wherever we happen to be. No one gave us a clear explanation at the start of our lives that the purpose of our existence is precisely to continue perfecting this house.

Being unaware of this, all we can do is follow the dictates of our past-programmed automatic responses, and resist our state of discomfort each in our own way.

Not only is this inner resistance hard to live with, but it also slows down the construction process considerably, if it doesn't stifle it altogether. We all know this simple but oh-so-powerful psychological law: "What we resist persists." By denying or resisting what is unfinished about the house, i.e. what is painful or "negative" within us, our "shadow", we are in fact feeding that shadow and making it last that much longer. That way we can unconsciously remain its prisoner for quite a while.

On the other hand, if we let go of resistance, and lovingly accept those "unfinished" parts of ourselves, we can joyfully get to work on cleaning up and putting the finishing touches to the house, and that way get things moving right along.

The moral teachings of the past were certainly useful as safeguards when human consciousness was not very highly developed and needed to be protected by "shoulds" and "should nots" and by a concept of good and bad. But the collective consciousness has evolved since then, and many people are now able to understand the dynamics of the evolutionary process, and consequently to fully grasp the fact that human beings are neither good nor evil. We all carry an extraordinary potential for doing "good", and the fact that this is not yet fully manifested is simply due to the fact that we are still progressing on the path towards the realisation of this "goodness". But this process has its laws, just as there are laws governing home construction. By recognising these laws, we can move much faster towards the realisation of our innermost being, instead of blaming ourselves for not being there yet.

2) Love thyself truly

Accepting our shadow, along with the confining structures of our unconscious—knowing that they have been both useful and temporary—not only liberates us from guilt, but enables us to experience the unfoldment of genuine self love, born of compassion, blossoming naturally within us. We know that while we still carry some negative characteristics (fears, selfishness, anger, etc.), it is not because we are at fault, bad, or not ok, **it is simply because we have suffered**. We have tried to protect ourselves with whatever resources we had available to us as we went through past trials. We could not do any better with the consciousness that was ours at the time.

Certainly self-love is emphasised in a lot of the literature currently available. But if this self-love is experienced at the level of our structures rather than at the level of genuine understanding that opens the heart, we stumble into a kind of false-love. That distorted self-love could then be used as a justification for anything that is triggered by our structures, and about which we remain unconscious. For example, the oral structure could use such encouragement towards self-love to justify its need to keep raising the bar of its emotional expectations; the masochist structure could use it to justify its anger towards those it perceives as oppressors; the psychopathic structure could use it to feed its pride; the rigid structure could reclaim it to justify its denial of feeling as a form of self-protection; and the schizoid structure could thus justify its need for isolation and **withdrawal. Loving ourselves does not mean letting our structures dictate how we live our lives**; it means understanding our limitations, accepting them with a lot of love and a firm resolve to work on defusing them, so that the energy locked into them can once again become available and put to better use.

Intelligent self-acceptance, as opposed to self-indulgence, is crucial for genuine inner transformation to occur for it allows us not to resist or feed our limitations, but rather to embrace them, thus transforming them. **Compassionate acceptance of our shadow is the key that opens the door to healing and to our own inner light.**

3) After all, it's only what they think

This knowledge can also be very helpful to stop being manipulated by what other people think of us. When people judge us and blame us for certain character flaws that we recognise and are presently working on, we will not let ourselves be demoralised by such messages. We will be able to respond, in a state of self-love and self-respect: "Yes, that's true, I still have that weakness, those fears or those alienating desires, etc., but I'm sorry, I'm just not finished." With this attitude, the impact of such judgements is dispelled.

Obviously we are not using this to try to justify or hang onto our weaknesses. We are simply aware that they are temporary in nature, and we accept them in order to better transcend them. As conscious and evolved human beings, our inner drive towards transformation remains active. We are therefore interested in liberating ourselves from such limitations, not because they are somehow not ok, but because we know that genuine happiness is contingent upon this liberation.

In addition, we know that others see us through the filter of their own structures. Consequently, we can distance ourselves all the more easily from all these put-downs, use those that seem justified as material for the construction work we are presently involved in and, with a serene and detached attitude, return to their sender those judgements that have nothing to do with us.

4) Compassion emerges naturally

We have often been urged not to judge, but to understand and accept others as they are. We have no problem with this as an intellectual principle. But putting this into practice on a daily basis is quite another matter! Indeed when we look at the way our defence systems were put in place over time, as we carry in us memories of betrayal, rejection, humiliation, abandonment, and all kinds of emotional traumas stemming from our relationships with others, it is no easy thing to practice a calm, serene and accepting attitude.

Yet we can now remind ourselves that, when some people around us behave in ways that are anything but harmonious, or in ways that could even be considered evil, they too carry their own history of suffering and "they also are not yet finished"! This vision triggers **a spontaneous feeling of compassion for others**, and therefore a state of readiness for greater tolerance and understanding. Our relationships are significantly and naturally improved. It becomes easier to forgive.

We can reinforce this tolerance and the distance we put between ourselves and our own reactions and judgements by remembering also that we are equally inclined to perceive others through our own defence systems, and that our day-to-day perception of things and other people is quite likely to be highly distorted. Because of these structures that clog the filter of our perception, we need to remind ourselves that "reality and our perception of reality can be two very different things."[4]

For example, if we happen to have a masochistic structure, we will tend to see instances of abuse of power everywhere we look; with a rigid structure, we will be very impatient with what appears to be disorderliness or lack of discipline, which may in fact be nothing more than the outward manifestation of flexibility and creativity; with an oral structure, we will tend to blame others for their apparent coldness, which may in fact be just the expression of inward contemplation; and with a psychopathic structure, we will experience an instant profound dislike towards any person who might upstage us.

So, when we catch ourselves leaning towards negative judgements, we will first turn our gaze inwardly to see where these judgements might be coming from. This can be an extremely effective form of daily spiritual workout to help us learn more about ourselves. Without knowing it, other people thus become our Teachers, enabling us to shed more light on the contents of our own consciousness. We must always remember that we perceive others not as they are, but rather as we are.

All of this leads to the natural practice of compassion and tolerance which are so badly needed in today's world, especially in the area of relationships.

5) Dynamic and fulfilling relationships

This broader perspective on human behaviour, our own and other people's, obviously creates the potential for a lot more harmony in our relationships. We can more easily appreciate each person for what he or she truly is, while observing with a tender smile the fits and starts of our own personalities. This knowledge helps to reduce our resistance to differences, and to live more readily in a state of acceptance and respect towards others. Tolerance is a natural doorway to brotherhood, understanding and genuine love.

In particular, when this state of openness exists within a **couple relationship**, it generates a quality of interaction that leads to genuine, accelerated evolution for both. First of all, we are compelled to acknowledge that our spouse is not God or the Divine Mother. He or she is a human being, with his or her personal history and defence patterns stemming from past suffering. Compassion for the other person in a couple is a powerful harmonising factor.

Instead of blaming the other person, we will more readily take responsibility for our own emotions, which is a most beneficial and liberating attitude in the context of an intimate relationship. So instead of expecting our partner to meet the needs and false desires of our structures and being upset with him or her for not doing so, we get to work on our own inner liberation.

Within the context of a couple relationship, we are confronted with the best and the worst of our deepest and most hidden realities. Consequently, this makes it an opportunity for major spiritual training, as we are being trained in our capacity for genuine love. No need to go frantically looking for a guru or to lead a hermit's life in a Himalayan cave. We have the Teacher right in front of us, and there is no escape! Consciously or not, he or she forces us to work directly on all the emotional mechanisms of our affective defence patterns, which are presently the strongest driving force in human behaviour and are the greatest hurdles to our spiritual enlightenment.

In this perspective, the couple relationship becomes a unique opportunity for authentic spiritual growth. We are a long way from romantic passion which is most often just an unconscious dance between defence systems, setting in motion the well known cycle of hopes, expectations and demands, followed by disappointment, despair and lack of understanding; finally ending up with a painful separation, with its usual chaos of suffering and negativity. With this new awareness, we can be much closer to having authentic relationships where mutual support, understanding, respect, and genuine tenderness are fertile ground for sharing the greatest of joys. This mindful openness makes it possible for the full power of love to come to life and generate miracles within relationships.

6) Simply being ourselves and having fun

Self-acceptance, including the acceptance of our shadow, opens the door to becoming progressively truer to ourselves, with great humility and flexibility. We can relax, knowing how futile it is to try to prove our so-called worth to the world. We are connected to the richness of our own inner world, either through a sense of the presence of our Self or through our awareness of our temporary limitations. We can ease into being truly ourselves, without fear, without conceit, with all the greatness of our higher Self and the good will of our personality.

10-4 Healing the Past

1) True healing and transformation – The need for synthesis

"Healing the past" is now readily accessible, and many healing techniques directly addressing the unconscious at the energetic level are available today. Yet despite our best efforts, we often get the impression that we are going around in circles. The reason is that when this work of liberating the past is in progress, something very important is missing. Indeed, to be effective, this work has to be done **simultaneously, at all levels of the human psyche**. This is what is often lacking in otherwise excellent approaches. Roughly speaking, the so-called spiritual approaches tend to focus almost exclusively on our inner light, while therapeutic approaches involve working almost exclusively on our shadow. We forget that all this should be seen as part of a cohesive whole. **Our consciousness cannot be divided into separate parts.** As we are going through a time of synthesis in all areas of human activities, inner and outer, we find that, here again, there is an urgent need to bring in the spirit of synthesis, and work at all three levels of our being, the conscious, the unconscious and the supraconscious.

In order to meet this need, it is extremely helpful to ensure that the work we do on defusing active memories is done in a **conscious context** that is as broad as possible (open-mindedness, understanding), and as free as possible from conscious thought patterns that block access to the unconscious. In doing so, we are putting into practice a principle that seems so simple and yet is so powerful and significant, i.e. **energy follows thought.**

The purpose of this first Volume is to provide a conscious context that is broad and solid enough to allow us to access the contents of our unconscious far more easily, no matter what method we subsequently use. Once this is established, then we can access much more easily and safely the contents of our unconscious to liberate it from any limiting aspects and harmonise it with all the other levels of our being.

However, **we cannot gain access to our unconscious directly from an ordinary conscious level**. Once the door is open, the contents of the unconscious must be addressed through different methods. The unconscious does not respond if we address it in our usual verbal mode. It has its own unique way of interpreting words. This is why the effectiveness of verbal methods is very limited for working at this level. On the other hand, there are two possible ways of establishing a direct access to the unconscious as a whole: either through direct energetic work, such as, for example, breathwork, hands-on healing and many other approaches, or through working with symbols and archetypes (symbolic processes that reach directly for the unconscious, often invoking the supraconscious as well). This is explored in more detail in *Free Your True Self 2*.

In my practice, I use several methods for healing the past at the energetic level, going directly to the memories imprinted in the unconscious and defusing them, but I am always careful to include the conscious aspect. This makes the process safe and provides quick results that are permanent.

If we carefully hang on to this perspective as we do our inner work, we can achieve a remarkable synthesis of all aspects of our being. In particular, we can tap into the full richness of our unconscious and thus enjoy all the natural vitality and power of the earth that it contains and that will prove to be a tremendous asset as we pursue our own inner realisation as well as our outer manifestation.

Many healing techniques directly addressing the unconscious at the energetic level are available today. Yet some of the most creditable therapies or the most inspiring spiritual disciplines lose much of their effectiveness if the conscious context in which they are practised is not appropriate. Indeed, despite our best efforts, we often get the impression that we are going around in circles. However, if we add to any one of these approaches an understanding of the structures of the unconscious from an evolutionary perspective, we find that the process of inner liberation is greatly accelerated. Indeed, **this knowledge is not exclusively applicable to any specific approach**. It simply offers a broader, more conscious context in which to do the work of transformation, no matter what method or teaching we choose to practice.

Understanding the coherence of our own mechanism of evolution and, **in this context**, developing a more compassionate knowledge of the structures of our unconscious, are the major keys to ensure that the process of healing and transformation is both authentic and effective. In my practice, I use several methods for healing the past at the energetic level, going directly to the memories imprinted in the unconscious and defusing them,[5] but I am always careful to include the conscious aspect. This makes the process safe and provides quick results that are permanent.

2) Choosing the right path and the best tools

By recognising our structures, we become more clearly aware of our strengths and weaknesses, and therefore more aware of the work to be done and the kind of help we might want to seek. We can thus make more **discriminating** choices among all the resources that are presently available. As a result, the books we read, the type of spiritual teaching we are drawn to, the therapists we select or the healing methods we resort to will naturally become far more effective. The choices we make are now more appropriate, and we get much quicker and more effective results.

This knowledge is also very useful if we happen to work as professional counsellors (therapists, psychologists, social workers, coaches, group leaders, etc.). The guidance we provide will be far more appropriate and specific, and therefore more effective.

10-5 Towards Genuine Spiritual Awakening

1) Moving away from "spiritual illusions"

There are many complex and highly abstract philosophies that talk about soul awakening and ultimate self-realisation. This complexity can be a trap where the mind is kept occupied with all sorts of mental gymnastics, some of them quite brilliant indeed, but whereby we unwittingly avoid facing the real work, which is to take a hard look at the state of the house: we get into lengthy discussions regarding blueprints, where the materials come from, environmental history, architectural relevance, we talk and talk. And in doing so, we avoid getting our hands dirty, but we don't build anything either, and our lives remain the same, day after day.

And yet, the proper path is not that hard to find. The real work is part of our day-to-day routine where, among other things, we can observe our ability to truly love, to get into right relationships, and to use our power for the benefit of all. Our progress in this work is not measured in terms of how articulate we may be when discussing spirituality, or how brilliant our intellectual abstractions may sound, but rather in terms of the quality of our service and the goodness we spread in our day-to-day existence. For this is where our level of consciousness is really tested, and where true spirituality comes to life.

Of course each defence system has its own way of reclaiming for its own ends the soul induced process of inner inquiry. We mentioned a few aspects of this in our detailed presentation of the five structures (see *Free Your True Self 2*, chapters 3 to 7). For example, the dynamics underscoring an individual's dependence on a guru, withdrawal into so-called "spiritual" dimensions, lack of openness or flexibility, excessive intellectualisation, "spiritual pride", etc., are major obstacles to genuine inner development. By bringing these under the spotlight of our consciousness, we can more readily transform them and thus clear the way to further growth.

When we can honestly recognise our own defence patterns as evidenced by our day-to-day behaviours—if we are willing to see them—we can dispel many "spiritual" illusions on our way to ultimate self-liberation, and free ourselves much more quickly from whatever impedes the full manifestation of our higher consciousness. The day-to-day reality of our lives, our material concerns and our relationships then become a genuine form of spiritual training that is challenging indeed in many ways, yet leads to **authentic transformation**.

2) Lightening the path to enlightenment

With this understanding and acceptance of the state of our human nature, we can carry on with our spiritual quest in a way that is far more authentic and infinitely lighter. Instead of hauling our shadow like a ball and chain without a glance in its direction, we can welcome its presence and **transform its dense**

mass of blocked energy into radiant vitality with each step we take. Thus our progress along the spiritual path can become a lighter, more joyful journey.

We then come to the realisation that the attention we put into bringing this "house" to the point of completion, into harmonising and healing our personality as it moves through the process of evolution, does anything but stall our spiritual progress. It actually allows us to **manifest in a concrete way the light, love and power of our higher consciousness in the world**. This is the very purpose of our existence. This house, born of the earth, becomes a cherished labour of love that is soon to be blessed.

10-6 The First and Last Freedom

In the end, this more conscious and loving form of self-knowledge leads the seeker to a most precious gift, i.e. **freedom**. And this freedom is ours on two levels:

—this perspective generates more freedom for self-healing and self-transformation. We can forget about dependency towards gurus or therapists. We will certainly still call upon wise teachers for help and guidance, but our inner maturity will allow us to use this assistance from a more autonomous standpoint, and to open our minds even more directly to **the guidance of our own higher consciousness**, our Inner Teacher;

—freedom will emerge as a major consequence of our inner work on our structures. The prison of our old selves based on our defence systems and the automatic responses they generate has turned each one of us into programmed, predictable robots that were consequently easily manipulated. Caught as we were in our automatic emotional and mental responses, we could not help reacting instead of acting, as soon as any situation triggered one of our memories. By liberating our consciousness from the grip of these automatic systems, we can really live in total freedom, for nothing and no one can manipulate someone who is in contact with his Soul.

When we recover this fundamental freedom, we can finally celebrate a wonderful reunion with the forgotten being we have always been, our higher consciousness, our True Self. In *Free Your True Self 2*, we will describe in greater detail the way we function at the level of the Higher Self, as well as its highly beneficial impact in our day-to-day existence.

We are definitely not destined to remain eternally caught up in our old patterns. When we free ourselves from them, we can live in a completely different state of consciousness. Though the outer conditions of our lives may remain the same, the way we respond to them emotionally, physically and mentally will not be the same. This occurs naturally because this is the way we are ultimately designed to function.

It is important to note that it is not necessary to "cultivate" the higher qualities of our Soul, even less to force these qualities upon ourselves (in any case, our unconscious would make us pay dearly for this intrusion). Unconditional love, compassion, creativity, joy, freedom and all these "positive" expressions of our being cannot be self-imposed. **They are already present in each human being.** All we need to do is to clear the way for them to emerge spontaneously from the depths of our heart. And this is indeed what happens when we heal and transform our unconscious structures. We are preparing a beautiful, warm and welcoming "house" so that our Higher Self will be happy to make it its home, bringing along its light, its joy and its loving presence. This house that was once a prison becomes a place of power for joyful creation, where Life is celebrated.

_____

[1] See *Free Your True Self 2*, by the same author, for more details on the human evolutionary process.

[2] Let us remember that the terms personality and ego (the aggregate of our three bodies, i.e. our mental, emotional and physical bodies) are interchangeable in this context.

[3] See *The Power of Free Will* and *The Master in Your Heart*, by the same author.

[4] See Annie Marquier, *The Power of Free Will*, Chapter 2.

[5] See *Free Your True Self 2*

chapter 11

Healing Our World

We are presently going through a major transition period in human history. An ever-increasing number of people are yearning for "a different world", a more serene, more harmonious, more loving, more abundant world for all, both inwardly and outwardly. This aspiration is just an indicator of a shift in consciousness that must take place in order to facilitate this planetary change.

We are in the process of coming out of millions of years of functioning at a "primary" level, where survival was the top priority, which in itself was perfectly appropriate in terms of the evolutionary process. However, a new era is now emerging in which our priorities will undergo a dramatic change. We have reached that pivotal point where we are still walking between two worlds. More and more people are sensing that something new is coming to life within them, as if they were ready to break out of an old skin.

The time has come to make a choice

We still have the choice either to hang onto the old, to our routines, our bogus sources of security and our hopes; to tune out of reality by losing ourselves in materialistic illusions or in emotional or intellectual spirituality, ultimately staying deaf and blind to what really needs to change; or we can inwardly tune into to this new reality, this **undeniable thrust of the Soul**.

The time to choose has now come, yet this is not necessarily an easy choice to make. Indeed the minute our Higher Self begins to emerge and tries to express its will, all our old mechanisms rear up in protest. We thus find ourselves caught between two opposing wills: the will of an ego that still rigidly sticks to its defence patterns and the will of our Higher Self, which loves its instrument and wants to use it to express all of its wonderful inherent qualities, in the unmitigated celebration of life and in the creation of love and beauty all around.

This distinction between the desires of our Higher Self and those of our personality is not always obvious...especially since the reality of desire has often been misunderstood in the context of spiritual teachings.[1] The point is not to eliminate desire, but to replace the personality's automatic desires, that generate only fleeting moments of happiness and extended periods of suffering, with the desires of our Higher Self which lead to lasting bliss and permanent well being.

In fact, as long as a human being remains at a lower stage of development, the impact of the Higher Self is relatively weak and the individual's life will be governed by fear and ego-generated desires of the ego, i.e. for the most part by unconscious defence systems. This is the usual pattern of behaviour of people who don't question the true meaning of their life.

But the impact of the presence of the Higher Self is much stronger for a lot of people right now. This is the point where an inner duality emerges between these two levels of will. **The entire spiritual process could be summed up as the transition from expressing the will of our personality to expressing the will of our Higher Self.** This transition is what a whole lot of people are presently experiencing. There is nothing mysterious about this. As our instrument—our personality—progressively opens up to the "divine" input from our Higher Self, it becomes naturally ready to leap to the next level of consciousness. The more we surrender to that higher level of consciousness, particularly by lovingly transforming our unconscious defence patterns, the more we experience a state of harmony within ourselves, with others and with Mother Earth. In this higher state, we recover the fullness of our vitality and creative power. We can thus achieve the goal of our True Self and make our contribution to the world spontaneously, in love and joyful service.

The time has come for humanity to make a choice

And yet, even if we manage to fully harmonise our lives at a personal level, we cannot ignore the fact that the world around us is presently in great pain. What can we do about it?

This is where we may realise that this personal choice of moving now from the old way of functioning to the new not only increases our own well being, but also has a major impact on our collective well being.

The fact is that **what goes on in the world is but the concrete expression, on the material plane, of the state of consciousness of humankind as a whole**. If all human beings lived at the level of their Higher Self in a state of brotherhood, respect, tolerance and compassion, our world would definitely be different than what it is today. But is there any way that billions of individuals could start putting such qualities into practice, i.e. is it ultimately possible to transform the level of consciousness of all humankind in just a few years? For time is running out.

The answer lies in a now well-known and scientifically authenticated natural phenomenon called morphic fields.[2] This phenomenon works according to the following principle (as described in *Free Your True Self 2*):

> "If, within a given species (mineral, plant, animal or human), a large enough number of individuals learn a specific subject of knowledge, the rest of the species becomes more receptive to this knowledge, and can acquire it far more quickly if not spontaneously. This phenomenon is no mere theory: it has been tested, not just in the notorious 'hundredth monkey' experiment, but in other scientific experiments as well involving mineral, plant and human species.

"When applied to mankind's change in consciousness, this phenomenon means that it is not necessary for each of the billions of people who make up the world's population to go through an individual consciousness change in order to see our general level of consciousness rise. It is not even necessary for a majority of individuals to experience a consciousness change, since this would already involve several billion people. What is needed, however, is that a certain number of individuals undergo such a change and create a so-called 'critical mass'. The moment this critical mass has been attained, a shift in consciousness for all humanity may occur within a few years or a few decades at the most. There lies our chance, our power.

"This information transmission phenomenon has been known to the great Masters of wisdom since the dawn of time. They have long been teaching that all human beings are linked together, particularly through what we call the Universal Mind. For instance, each time an individual has a love-inspired thought or action, he or she feeds the love that is latent in every other human being. The same can be said of all states of consciousness, from the lowest to the highest. Each time we heal memories from the past, this healing resonates in the collective unconscious and fosters deliverance in others. Every time an individual gains a little more mastery on the personality level and develops a stronger connection to his or her Higher Self, this level of mastery becomes available to the rest of humanity."

Thus, through our own inner work, by becoming more and more receptive to the guidance of our Higher Self—in particular by setting ourselves free of our own unconscious defence systems—not only do we generate more peace and joy in our personal lives, but we also foster the emergence of more peace and light on Earth as a whole. **In healing ourselves, we heal the world.**

This is not just some New Age fantasy. This is a very real energetic phenomenon with a major impact. It can even be extraordinarily potent if there is a large enough number of people to form that critical mass. Therein lies our best chance—maybe even the only one—to save humankind.

And there is no need for us to start a crusade or another war to save the world. Outward action is certainly totally desirable, as there is in fact a tremendous amount of work to do. But before we act, we need to be as clear as possible in terms of what truly motivates us. For it is a fact that **the outcomes generated by any action are contingent upon the true source of that action**. If the source of our daily actions is our defence systems, then all we are doing is reinforcing them in our personal lives and in the collective unconscious. If the source is our Higher Self, then we reinforce the power of love in the world in thousands of ways, no matter what our actions may be.

The time has come for humankind as a whole to create and to live in a different world, a different reality. The reality of the soul, or Higher Self, is not a myth, nor is it a philosophy or a spiritual daydream that is out of touch with the world. This reality has the potential to express itself in a concrete way now on our planet, in the midst of all human activities. Fear, separation and misery can disappear. If enough of us succeed in transforming our unconscious defence patterns in order to open our hearts to the power, the wisdom and the compassion of our Higher Self, then our international defence systems, which are the collective expression of our fears, can disappear so we can establish the kind of world we all yearn for—a world of understanding, respect, brotherhood and freedom for all human beings.

We already have the necessary means to accomplish this. All that is missing is the consciousness required to use them. Peace on Earth is not primarily a product of political organisation or external events. **The actual deeper roots of a world of peace lie in the level of consciousness of humankind.** All the rest is just a series of consequences thereof.

Thanks to the natural phenomenon of morphic fields, by liberating our True Self, by aligning our lives and actions with its wisdom, we have the potential, at the start of this twenty-first century, to play our part not only in improving our own quality of life, but to be instrumental in bringing about a major shift in consciousness at the collective level. Our Mother Earth can then become a place of celebration, freedom and abundance for all human beings. This is still within our reach. **The inner freedom of each of us is the powerful catalyst that will generate freedom for all of us.**

A new world is in the process of emerging, a world never before seen as the human race has never reached this stage of evolution; a world that we will create **by becoming conscious of what we have been, what we are and what we can become**, by putting our Higher Self in charge of our lives so that our very existence and our world will be the expression of this higher intelligence, of this infinite Love.

We are being handed an incredible opportunity. Our time has come.

---

[1] See *Free Your True Self 2*

[2] Please refer in particular to Rupert Sheldrake, *A New Science of Life*, Park Street Press, Vermont, 1995.

Epilogue

The Dawn

At the first light of day, a dove gazes from the top of the mountain at the darkness withdrawing from the valley below. The gentle light of a new day begins to rise. What seemed to be lost or even non-existent in the dark now comes into view. The light grows brighter, revealing paths, rivers and forests, their colours growing ever richer, more wonderful and iridescent. The bird plunges downward, discovering fields of flowers, with animals full of curiosity joyfully frolicking about in the meadows and through the woods. All the life that had slumbered in the dark of night is being reborn, its energy renewed, richer for these hours spent in darkness. This is the homecoming into the light at the end of the journey through the night. Life that was gone now returns; it is time to celebrate the dawn of a new world.

Other books by Annie Marquier

Free Your True Self 2: The Power of the Soul

We are presently going through a crucial time of transition in human history. In this transition each of us has the opportunity to experience a deep inner transformation leading to a completely new way of experiencing life. Annie Marquier's books **Free Your True Self** offer clear, precise and powerful tools to foster this transformation.

While Volume 1 – *Releasing Your Unconscious Defence Patterns* – extends our self-knowledge on the nuts-and-bolts level of our personality structures, **Free Your True Self 2 –** *The Power of the Soul* provides a broader context in which to hold this information. Founded on Annie Marquier's solid background of psychological and spiritual knowledge based on the Ageless Wisdom, this second volume presents a clear and profound understanding of the mechanisms of human consciousness and of the inner process of transformation. Using the broad perspective of the evolutionary process grounded with numerous life stories and practical examples, this book provides highly effective and transformative insights. In particular it sharpens our understanding of our way of functioning on the basis of two major dynamics: an old one, very familiar, which is a source of little satisfaction and, most of the time, stress, worry and suffering, and a new one, which generates freedom, power and joy in our lives. This new approach allows the concrete integration of the highly beneficial power of the soul in our day to day existence, enabling us to create true happiness, not only for ourselves but also for the whole planet.

In this second volume, Annie Marquier offers a unique synthesis of spiritual and psychological approaches which allows us **to ground the process of inner work in concrete terms**, and at the same time open our heart and spirit to a new vision of our destiny as a human race.

An invaluable book to meet the challenges of our times, **Free Your True Self 2 -** *The Power of the Soul* provides fundamental keys to free ourselves from thousands of years of conditioning and be again the powerful, joyful and loving person we always wanted to be, our True Self.

ISBN 1-84409-061-2

Publication fall 2005 • Available from your local bookstore
or order directly from www. findhornpress.com

Planned for 2006:

The Power of Free Will

In a world of uncertainty and stress, this book offers a new perspective from which to experience life, bringing back inner strength, harmony and peace in all areas of our lives — a strong new paradigm to recover one's essential creative power and the deeper meaning of one's existence.

First exploring the filter of perception of human consciousness; its function; its working mechanism; and its impact on the way we experience life, *The Power of Free Will* then proposes a change of paradigm: leaving behind the victim paradigm so ingrained in our collective psyche, to find through the new paradigm of "responsibility-attraction-creation" that we really have the power to choose what to make of all the situations life offers to us. This is not a new idea, but the way it is usually presented leads to a lot of misunderstanding. To make this paradigm clear and useful, Annie Marquier bases her work on a deep understanding of the mechanisms of human consciousness stemming from the Ageless Wisdom teachings as well as on a compassionate and comprehensive observation of human psychology. These two aspects give the paradigm all its strength and worth, on both a philosophical and practical level.

This book bears a very practical message with a lot of stories and examples of daily life. It is a powerful tool for a major switch in personal and collective consciousness.

" The Power of Free-Will is a comprehensive and powerful presentation of the many implications of the basic truth that we are each responsible for ourselves, our lives and our choices. This profound work illustrates with countless stories and examples the damaging results of assuming the posture of the victim in relation to our life experience. This work convincingly proves that by understanding and transforming our emotional states we then have the power to freely choose a better future for ourselves, humanity and all life on our planet."
—Gordon Davidson, Director, Center for Visionary Leadership,
co-author of *Builders of the Dawn* and *Spiritual Politics*

For information on courses, seminars and conferences conducted
by **Annie MARQUIER**, please contact:
Institut du Développement de la Personne
P.O. Box 1074, Knowlton, Qc
JOE 1VO Canada
Tel.: (450) 242-1961 - Fax: (450) 242-2610
Web Site: **www.idp.qc.ca**
E-mail: info@idp.qc.ca

For further information about the Findhorn Foundation and the Findhorn Community, please contact:

Findhorn Foundation

The Visitors Centre
The Park, Findhorn IV36 3TZ, Scotland, UK
tel 01309 690311
enquiries@findhorn.org
www.findhorn.org

For a complete Findhorn Press catalogue, please contact:

Findhorn Press

305a The Park, Findhorn
Forres IV36 3TE
Scotland, UK
tel 01309 690582
fax 01309 690036
info@findhornpress.com
www.findhornpress.com